Michael Sharwood Smith

Aspects of Future Reference in a Pedagogical Grammar of English

FORUM LINGUISTICUM

Herausgegeben von Professor Dr. Christoph Gutknecht

Band 19

Michael Sharwood Smith

Aspects of Future Reference in a Pedagogical Grammar of English

PETER LANG
Frankfurt am Main · Bern · Las Vegas

Michael Sharwood Smith

Aspects of Future Reference in a Pedagogical Grammar of English

PETER LANG
Frankfurt am Main · Bern · Las Vegas

CIP-Kurztitelaufnahme der Deutschen Bibliothek

Sharwood Smith, Michael

Aspects of future reference in a pedagogical grammar of English. - Frankfurt am Main, Bern, Las Vegas: Lang, 1977.
   (Forum linguisticum; Bd. 19)
   ISBN 3-261-02384-8

This work, in substantially the same form, was accepted in 1974 at Adam Mickiewicz University, Poznań in partial fulfilment of the degree of Doctor of Humanities.

ISBN 3-261-02384-8

Auflage 300 Ex.

© Verlag Peter Lang GmbH, Frankfurt am Main 1978

Alle Rechte vorbehalten.
Nachdruck oder Vervielfältigung, auch auszugsweise, in allen Formen wie Mikrofilm, Xerographie, Mikrofiche, Mikrocard, Offset verboten.

Druck: Fotokop Wilhelm Weihert KG, Darmstadt
Titelsatz: Fotosatz Aragall, Wolfsgangstraße 92, Frankfurt am Main.

To Ewa

TABLE OF CONTENTS

	Page
PREFACE	6
INTRODUCTION	7

Chapter One
LANGUAGE PEDAGOGY AND GRAMMAR 9

Chapter Two
FUTURE REFERENCE PAST AND PRESENT 56

Chapter Three
A PEDAGOGICAL GRAMMAR OF FUTURE REFERENCE 87

BIBLIOGRAPHY 108

SUMMARY OF CONTENTS 119

PREFACE

Since this work was completed, in 1974, the writer has written a number of articles and papers developing some of its main themes. The psychological dimension of applied linguistics, and in particular of pedagogical language descriptions is elaborated on in Sharwood Smith 1976a and (forthcoming) a. The analysis of time reference is extended on a somewhat less "applied" level to cover present and past reference in Sharwood Smith (forthcoming) b, that is, within the two-predicate analysis mentioned in Chapter Three. The reader may usefully compare this work with another dissertation on future reference verbs in English written independently by Wekker (Wekker 1976), which is data-based, eclectic (along the lines of Quirk et al. 1974, c.f. Wekker, op.cit:21) but which, although written with pedagogical needs in mind, is not concerned with the theory of pedagogical grammar. One notable feature of this work is that the case for a future tense in English is argued for.

M.S.S. 1977.

REFERENCES

SHARWOOD SMITH, M.A. (1976a) "Pedagogical Grammar" in Interlanguage Studies Bulletin - Utrecht 1:45-58.

..... (forthcoming) a. "Applied Linguistics and the Psychology of Instruction" in the Proceedings of the 6th Neuchâtel Colloquium to be published by Indiana Linguistics Club.

..... (forthcoming) b. "More on Tense and Time Reference" in Papers and Studies in Contrastive Linguistics (ed. J. Fisiak).

WEKKER, H.Chr. (1976) The Expression of Future Time in Contemporary British English. Amsterdam: North Holland.

INTRODUCTION

The aim of this thesis, as expressed in the title: <u>Aspects of Future Reference in a Pedagogical Grammar of English</u>, may be subdivided into two interdependent parts. The first part comprises the investigation of certain ways in which native speakers of English--the British Standard--refer to the future. The future is here defined as that portion of the time dimension that the speaker conceptualises as being "after the present" in relation to the time of utterance. The approach will be <u>notional</u>, and the justification for this approach will be given in the first chapter. With regard to linguistic forms, most attention will be given to <u>verbal forms</u> as these seem to be the most important markers of future reference. Future time adverbials will, of course, be discussed in relation with verb forms. The purpose of this thesis will be to concentrate on an overall conceptual framework and it is recognised that the treatment of individual forms such as <u>will</u> alone could easily be the topic for an extra thesis.

The second part comprises an investigation of the problem of how to design <u>pedagogical grammars</u>, that is, grammars written explicitly for the benefit of language learners. Up till recently, teaching grammars have been conceived of either as "simplifications" of more theoretical works or as practical collections of grammatical information based on the writer's own experience of teaching rather than a straight application of pure linguistic research. In the present writer's view, the time is ripe for attempting not only to formulate a set of principles for writing such grammars (rather than writing them on some intuitional ad-hoc basis) but also for actually attempting to describe portions of the language to see how these principles might work. This thesis has chosen the area of future reference as testing ground for a set of principles formulated in the first chapter.

Future reference is a dangerous and controversial area. Poutsma, talking of *will* and *shall* alone, speaks of a maze through which the native speaker seems miraculously to be able to walk with a kind of "sixth organ" (1928:11) which enables him to know exactly when to use them. Jespersen spoke of "the various more or less unsettled ways whereby many languages find expression for the future" (Jespersen 1909, revised 1961:24) and attributes this inherent complexity to the fact that the future is by its nature uncertain. *Will* and *shall*, the arch-criminals in this area, provoke the applied linguist R.A. Close to admit the "tangle of idiomatic and conflicting usage amongst native speakers". This thesis will be a modest attempt to find a way out of this tangle.

CHAPTER ONE

1.0. LANGUAGE PEDAGOGY AND GRAMMAR

1.1. Language Pedagogy

Language pedagogy may be defined as the investigation of the factors that effect language teaching. The investigator is responsible for interpreting the results of his investigations in a principled way and constructing theories that will a. improve our understanding of the teaching and learning of languages and b. provide an explicit set of principles from which teaching material and syllabuses may be evolved. Stated this way, language pedagogy seems to be a relatively new discipline (cf. Krzeszowski 1970, Sharwood-Smith 1972 and Corder 1973). However, this field of investigation is actually centuries old and many apparently "new" ideas in language pedagogy and pedagogy in general have their parallels in concepts expressed in earlier epochs. For instance, Hoole, a seventeenth century writer, once said:

> Till a memory and understanding go hand in hand a child learns nothing to any purpose.
>
> (Hoole, in Kelly 1969:315)

which sounds remarkably like a contemporary attack on rote learning. David Ausubel, for example, stressing meaningful learning as opposed to parrotlike learning of information without any conscious understanding (rote learning) says:

> When we deliberately attempt to influence cognitive structures so as to maximise meaningful learning and retention, we come to the heart of the educative process.
>
> (Ausubel 1968:126)

We may be no nearer to ideal solutions in language pedagogy than writers like Hoole or Comenius, but recent work in sociology, psychology and linguistics allows us to systematise our knowledge and bring it in line with contemporary scientific research.

1.2. Language Pedagogy and Grammar

The most immediate concern in this thesis is with <u>pedagogical grammar</u>. There are different interpretations of this term, and it is important to clear up possible sources of misunderstanding. Firstly, there is, as Corder points out, the interpretation which includes all teaching materials regardless of function, which must be distinguished from "the presentation of information about language for teaching purposes" (Corder 1973:154). This latter definition excludes the exploitation of information in the preparation of exercises and drills and also for drawing up syllabuses. However, it will be argued that the presentation should facilitate such exploitation. If we adapt this definition as a starting point, there are several further distinctions to be made.

Firstly, we will be dealing with the larger scale type of grammar and not with small segments separated out for units in teaching material. Naturally the smaller segments should be derived from the larger scale descriptions.

Secondly, information which is primarily lexical may be excluded with the proviso that a pedagogical grammar should aim to establish as many links as possible between descriptions of the system and descriptions of small open set items in the lexicon. Thus the established distinction between the dictionary and the grammar is, in principle, maintained.

Thirdly, we may make a distinction between generalised and specialised grammars. Contrastive pedagogical grammars on a parallel with such grammars as The Grammatical Structures of English and Italian (Agard and Di Pietro 1965) would come under the category of specialised grammars. So would language descriptions designed for learners of a particular profession, or any subset of learners with a particular well-defined purpose for learning the language.

Finally, the distinction may be made between reference books in the accepted sense of the word and teaching grammars where the concept of reference would include not only casual use but also the more intensive use of the grammar for developing syllabuses and teaching material. In the present writer's opinion the most interesting, useful and genuinely pedagogical grammar would be the latter type. Such a grammar would be primarily for the advanced student, the teacher, the coursebook writer and the syllabus designer, i.e. the kind of user that Jespersen was doubtless thinking of when he wrote A Modern English Grammar (1909-1949). From this type of grammar, simpler versions can be evolved providing only the "essentials", or more specialised versions for specific "consumers".

The question now arises as to what considerations should be taken into account when constructing a pedagogical grammar. Recent works, particularly in the United States, have placed most of the emphasis on the linguistic (theoretical) input to the grammar. Less attention has been paid to other potential input sources and to adjusting the grammar to cope with feedback from the users. In short, pedagogical grammar has not always been sufficiently consumer-oriented. The immediate application of structural linguistic description in the classroom, after an initial period of enthusiasm from linguists, behaviourist psychologists and dazzled language teachers, proved disappointing in its results. The effects did not stop with the introduction of transformational-generative principles. Lawler and Selinker (1971) attack Owen Thomas (cf. Thomas 1965) for bringing linguistics unadulterated to the classroom and suggest that a more empirical approach is necessary, going from what is observed in the classroom and the intuitions of language teachers. They oppose Thomas' idea that a pedagogical grammar should simply follow "the best scientific grammar available" (Thomas 1965:5): this is simply teaching linguistics rather than language.

Although a large part of the grammar is clearly going to owe a great deal to theoretical linguistic research, there are psychological (and sociological) considerations which may lead us to view aspects of the theoretical description as irrelevant and even misleading. As Corder says:

> The problem of devising an efficient pedagogical grammar is (...) more a psycholinguistic than a theoretical linguistic one. The form our pedagogical grammar takes will be dependent upon what we believe to be the psychological processes involved in language learning.
>
> (Corder 1973:331-2)

Chomsky's distinction between competence and performance has been found to be misleading both by psychologists who would like to apply it to the study of language behaviour and sociologists who see the definition of competence as too narrow (cf. Greene 1972:94ff. and 194-6 and Hymes 1970). The attempt by Charles Fries to establish form classes in grammar independent of meaning (following Bloomfield) and labelling the classes by numbers seems to hinder rather than facilitate the learning of language which, after all, language learners need primarily to convey meaning. The many abstract technical aspects of both Bloomfieldian and Chomskyan analysis cannot be related easily to language learning situations.

There is another disadvantage of theoretical linguistics for pedagogical application. The attempt to create elegant scientific theories prompts many theoreticians to <u>restrict their field</u> to the extent that they do not deal with aspects of language that are of vital concern to the learner. The "best scientific grammar" may turn out to be the least helpful and the writer of a pedagogical grammar may well turn to linguists like Jespersen who have been criticised for inconsistency and vagueness but who have had a more comprehensive view of what linguists should aim at describing. Typically, it is these more comprehensive linguists who show a sympathetic interest in language teaching and even take part in writing teaching grammars. Even in his <u>Philosophy of Grammar</u> (1924), Jespersen showed a concern for relating what he called "higher grammar" to school grammar (Jespersen 1924:356), and it is there that he stated that his <u>Modern English Grammar</u> was for advanced students of English. Almost fifty years after Jespersen's _Philosophy_, we find a reaction to the reductionist tendencies of orthodox Chomskyan linguistics in the form of the new school of generative semantics (reinterpreting Chomsky). Generative semanticists also aim for a more comprehensive view taking in those aspects which interest the language learner. Robin Lakoff said:

> There are areas of linguistic competence that cannot be described in any theory that does not allow an integration of information about the context in which the discourse takes place--sometimes erroneously referred to as the "real world" as opposed to "linguistically relevant" situation--and the purely linguistically relevant information the sentence seems to convey: superficial syntax, choice of lexical items, and semantics aside from contextually relevant meaning elements.
>
> (R. Lakoff 1972:909)

Generative semantics is in an even more fragmentary state than orthodox transformational grammar and yet the language teacher may find more of direct relevance in the former than the latter. Not surprisingly, R. Lakoff, like Jespersen, has a sympathetic attitude to language teachers. In fact, she has suggested that applied linguists, i.e. those working in language pedagogy, would do well to cooperate more closely:

> Applied linguists know where second language learners make mistakes and what kind of errors they make (...). Thus in this area, as in many others, progress can best be made by theoretical and applied linguists if they will work together as equal partners.
>
> (R. Lakoff 1973)

This contrasts sharply with what Chomsky had to say to language teachers at the Northeast Conference on the Teaching of Foreign Languages (1965) where he declared himself both to be not competent to speak on language teaching and sceptical about the significance of recent advances in either linguistics or psychology (Allen and Van Buren 1971:152-3). The implication (which was perhaps salutary at the time) was that contemporary linguistics and language teaching should get on with their separate business until a real reason appears for them to relate their fields. This would confirm the fact at least that orthodox Chomskyan linguistics will not provide the best scientific grammar for the pedagogical grammarian. It would also lead us to suppose that <u>eclecticism</u> is at present the only practical solution and furthermore that in being eclectic we should concentrate on those grammars which have something to say about meaning, usage, performance, context and all those aspects which are covered by theoreticians who have <u>not</u> been credited with producing the best scientific grammars.

The principle of eclecticism involves an obvious danger in that it can easily throw us back to the situation where we are simply making the best of a bad job. Linguists like Chomsky do not deny the theoretical justification for basing pedagogical grammar on some "higher" description. They simply say that theoretical works are too fragmentary and are not likely to result in full-scale descriptions anyway. Hypothetically it still remains the ideal course of action to adopt what might be termed the <u>parasitic</u> approach to pure linguistics and accept as much of theoretical linguistics as is deemed possible. We pick and choose as we can and fill in the gaps with material and intuitions of our own. We arrive at what may be called patchwork grammar. There is, however, another alternative which has already been hinted at, namely, to take a <u>selective</u> approach. That is to say, we adopt the view of applied science which has its own rationale for dealing with theoretical insights and gives due importance to other considerations outside the mother discipline. Without wishing to stretch the analogy too far, the example of transformational grammarian borrowings from logic, philosophy and mathematics might be cited as examples of the selective approach to related fields. Applied science has some justifiable independence from the theoretical "pure" science that seems to give rise to it (cf. Lawler and Selinker, Ausubel 1968:15ff.). What this amounts to saying is that language pedagogy including its major component, pedagogical grammar (or "pedagogical linguistics", cf. Sharwood-Smith 1972), has its own set of principles. Thus pedagogical grammars should be constructed in a principled way according to criteria independent of pure linguistic studies. We may accordingly summarise the two approaches in diagram form as follows:

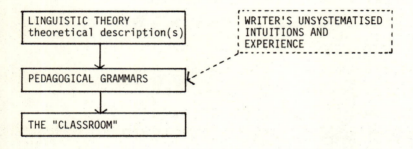

Fig. 1. The parasitic-eclectic approach

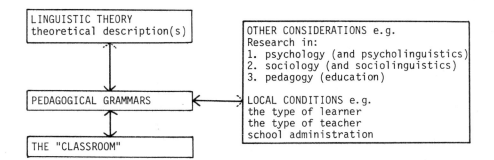

Fig. 2. The selective approach

(two-way arrows represent potential reciprocal relationships allowing for feedback).

Both approaches are limited by the fragmentary nature of current linguistic theory and theoretical descriptions. The selective approach however is to be preferred because:

a. it provides systematic means for choosing amongst different linguistic theories and descriptions (see "OTHER CONSIDERATIONS").

b. it allows for the fact that a pedagogical grammar needs to have a strong psychological (and perhaps sociological) foundation.

c. it is more flexible in that it allows for feedback from the classroom, which can be assessed from more than a linguistic point of view.

These two approaches should of course be seen as a simplification of the real situation and are simply used here to illustrate the principles involved.

1.3. Grammar: Internal Design

In accordance with established practice in twentieth century grammar, pedagogical grammar should:

1. give <u>rules describing actual usage</u> rather than prescriptive utterances which have no relation to actual usage.
2. be <u>synchronic</u> in that it describes contemporary language and not archaic usage unless specifically aimed at readers of literature.
3. be designed in a principled way.

This conforms with strictures found in any general work on linguistics today, e.g. Halliday, McIntosh and Strevens, Lyons 1968, Crystal 1971, Wilkins 1972. One of the more unsettled issues is the relationship between <u>form</u> and <u>meaning</u>. Most people would agree that the study of language consists of relating form and meaning. The question is whether we should analyse language starting from its outer form to see how meanings are expressed by forms. To take a more specific example, would we place <u>will</u> together with other items that are formally similar, i.e. have similar syntactic behaviour (<u>shall</u>, <u>may</u>, <u>must</u>, <u>should</u>, <u>would</u>, <u>might</u>, etc.) or should a language analysis place <u>will</u> with other items that express similar meanings (<u>shall</u>, <u>going to</u>, <u>be bound to</u>, <u>be to</u>, <u>tomorrow</u>, <u>next Tuesday</u>, etc.)? Furthermore, should a description make a rigid separation between formal and meaning aspects or should the analysis combine them within one system? The former seems more elegant and less likely to create confusion. The latter seems more realistic (cf. Crystal 1971:239).

Traditional grammars including the scholarly grammars of writers like Jespersen and Kruisinga have been labelled, often pejoratively (or at least in a way that "damns with faint praise"), as <u>notional</u>. In fact, a genuine notional grammar has not been produced by any twentieth century linguist, and one has to go back to the logical grammars of the eighteenth century to find analyses that were fully based on extralinguistic assumptions - in this case logic. The real criticism of notional grammars was that they were not uniformly based on formal linguistic grounds but, on the contrary, mixed up notional and formal distributional categories without good reason. For this reason they have been labelled as "unscientific" or "rather vague" and "largely subjective" (F. Palmer 1965:6). These grammars may in part be defended, as Van Buren points out (1967), by noting:

1. that the device of defining most parts of speech syntactically and leaving the noun (and sometimes the verb) to be defined notionally did avoid the danger of circularity
2. that syntactic form classes arrived at distributionally are remarkably similar to traditional parts of speech.

The first American structuralist reaction to the vagueness of the so-called notional grammars was at first extreme. Following Bloomfield's stricture that meaning was not to be analysed by linguists (Bloomfield 1933:162), Charles Fries (1940, 1952) arrived at a set of distributional categories of the slot-and-filler type which were labelled numerically (e.g. form classes I-IV) and made no reference to any notions whatsoever. Noam Chomsky (1965, etc.) brought meaning back into linguistics but concentrated mainly on establishing the syntactic component of the grammar, leaving the semantic component specified only in outline. Only in more recent years, as was mentioned previously, has work been done starting from a semantic base (making no rigid distinction between syntax and semantics), e.g. in generative semantics.

Post-Jespersonian developments in Europe have been less extreme and there seems to have been an underlying tendency to look for notional justification for grammatical categories, while at the same time ceding to the practicality of following the more readily discernable regularities of syntax. There has never been a total rejection of meaning. Jespersen himself discusses the different ways of setting out language description going from outer to inner or vice versa (<u>O--- I</u> or <u>I--- O</u>, cf. Jespersen 1924:39). He includes meaning as the third criterion for setting up item classes (form, function and meaning). However, in practice he tends to begin with the outer form and progress to statements of meaning. Occasionally we get sections which are purely notional, such as the "notional survey" in Chapter XXII in the third volume of <u>A Modern English Grammar</u> dealing with the English verb where he hopes to "examine how far and in what way they (universal notions of time) are expressed by the English verb" (p. 352). On the matter of whether there should be separate sections in the grammar Jespersen (1923:40) disagrees with Sweet's approval of this idea. He concedes (Jespersen 1923:41) that we have to keep these things apart as much as possible, but "it must be our endeavour to frame our divisions in the most natural means possible and to avoid unnecessary repetitions by means of cross-references". By adopting the more realistic and natural approach, Jespersen chooses the scientifically suspect path and exposes himself to the criticisms mentioned above. However, later

European attempts have never quite deserted this ambivalent approach although there have been attempts to make language analysis more systematically elegant, that is, to formalise language with more precision and economy. Kruisinga, according to Zandvoort "made an audacious attempt to base the analysis of the structure of English on a strictly formal principle" (Zandvoort 1970:95) but went too far and ignored the fact that "we need the application of notional grammar as a check on formal grammar" (Zandvoort 1970:95). Kruisinga was not in fact unaware of the problem as can be shown in the following quotation:

> Instead of considering what are the meanings expressed by the forms of sentence structure that are current in a given language it is possible to, and instructive, to consider what are the forms that are available in a language to express certain meanings.
>
> (Kruisinga 1925:330-1)

However, a little later he indicates his preference for the formal approach:

> The general opinion seems to remain unshaken that it is rather the task of logical grammar to supplement formal grammar and to gather up the threads in cases where formal grammar is compelled to separate them.
>
> (Kruisinga 1925:339)

Thus Kruisinga comes near to sweeping the meaning problem under the carpet and, in effect, it is argued here, leaves the job of notional grammar to the applied linguist who has serious grounds for trying to establish one (see 1.4., for example).

European linguists have always shown a concern for finding a place for meaning in their analyses although the general emphasis has been for finding a general theory that accounts for the distributional facts of language. Firthian and Hallidayan systematic grammar has nonetheless included some account of the meaning function of language, in particular the links between forms and the communicative context (cf. Firth 1951, Halliday 1961, 1970). John Lyons has been concerned with establishing internal systems of meaning (cf. Lyons 1963, 1968). And F. Palmer, in basing his analysis of English verbs on formal principles still stresses the importance of meaning as a way of arriving at some formal categories:

> All linguists today are agreed upon the necessity for a formal approach to grammatical analysis.
>
> (Palmer 1965:6)

> A formal statement is formal as long as the criteria are formal, the definitions are made in terms of form. The extent to which semantic criteria have <u>led</u> to a particular statement is quite irrelevant.
>
> (Palmer 1965:7)

Linguists of the Prague school, on lines roughly parallel to those who are related to the Firthian school and its later developments, show and interest in relating language to its communicative function. A. Mensiková (Fried 1972) outlined the fundamental principles of the Prague school stressing this aspect. By proceeding from communication function to form the Prague approach corresponds to the viewpoint of the speaker, in real life, who "has to find linguistic form for what he wishes to express" (Fried 1972:44). Actually, the same point is made by Jespersen but within the context of his suggestion for two interrelated grammars. I--- O and O--- I correspond to the situations faced by the speaker and hearer respectively (Jespersen 1924:46). Mathesius, the founder of the Prague school, found Jespersen's approach in reality biased towards what would here be the hearer's point of view (the formal approach). He criticised Jespersen's Essentials of English Grammar (1933) because in his opinion it failed to go deep enough beneath the complexity of outward phenomena. While giving us fairly complete information about the syntactic and morphological structure of English, the book omits what Mathesius calls the onomatological aspect of English, that is, its linguistic repertoire of names together with the application of this repertoire to concrete acts of speech. Every linguistic act involves choosing elements of reality and their linguistic correlates (names) and organising these into sentences. The linguistic investigator should start from the communicative needs of the speaker-- "from functional necessities to formal means by which they are satisfied" (Fried 1972:308ff.).

We still wait in vain for the grammar which promises the teacher what seems to be most relevant to his needs. There is no doubt that this need is felt. R.A. Close (1962) writes of the necessity the learner is faced with to know how the various forms of the language are used to convey the meanings wishes to express. Until he has learned from experience he must go to the dictionary or:

> that part of grammar which is concerned not so much with facts as with DISTINCTIONS OF THOUGHT, PERSONAL ATTITUDES and POINTS OF VIEW.
>
> (Close 1962:13)

The stress on the importance of the notional aspect of language for the learner is repeated by H.V. George, writing about the teaching grammatical features:

> Every effort should be made to effect a conceptual basis for each feature.
>
> (George 1972:19)

And J.W. Tober, speaking at the 1972 conference of applied linguistics (AILA, Copenhagen) calls for a pedagogical grammar that seems to relate closely to the ambitions of the Prague school:

> A descriptive model which meets the needs of applied linguistics must be based on the dynamic aspects of language use, that is to say, on the operations that produce the linguistic structure itself, because the skills involved in language use are essentially sets of operations and not results such as structure, form ...
>
> (Tober 1972)

What is required here is in fact what Chomsky would call a performance model of grammar (Chomsky 1965:9, 15 and 198). Tober explains that language use consists of syntagmatic operations, cutting up reality and assigning a place in the sentence (subject, verb, object) to each distinctive unit, and paradigmatic operations

> which provide the meanings to which the speaker is referring to, e.g., choosing the right lexical or formal unit out of a paradigm in order to refer accurately to the reality to be expressed.
>
> (Tober 1972)

This is reminiscent of Mathesius' onomatological function. It highlights the speaker's point of view. It is this point of view that applied linguists, and teachers in general, would like to see given more emphasis in the design of pedagogical grammars.

David Wilkins in <u>Linguistics in Language Teaching</u> (1972a), while fully recognising the need for a notional dimension in pedagogical grammar,

carries the ambivalent attitude to form versus meaning which is held by
European general linguists, into the field of language teaching. While
conceding that a comprehensive view of the language must account for
both form and meaning, he states that a semantic-notional approach will
produce an orientation in language teaching
> which denies the pedagogic benefits of using a language's formal
> regularities in the organisation of teaching.
>
> (Wilkins 1972a:19)

Meaning is not susceptible to an empirical approach due to its complex
nature (Wilkins 1972:17ff.). Yet Wilkins himself has worked on a notional
syllabus for the Council of Europe (cf. Wilkins 1972b). He states here
that
> language descriptions provide the input to the creation of teaching
> materials, so that the materials inevitably reflect the types of
> description on which they are based.

We may infer from this that the notional syllabus which he outlines presupposes a language description built along notional lines. Yet in his
book (1972a), he is much more cautious about surrendering grammatical
design to notional categories. Here it is referred to as the "more
radical approach" (Wilkins 1972b:146) and applicable only to situations
where the learners are advanced and have well-defined communicative aims.
There is no reason, however, to accept this more conservative point of
view and refrain from extending our knowledge of the notional aspect of
language in order to arrive at a much more systematic, explicit idea of
what they are. We should develop the idea of a two-component grammar
with elaborate cross-referencing, keeping in mind the attempt to devise
categories (formal and notional) which facilitate useful revealing

statements to be made in the other component (formal or notional). As
Wilkins himself points out (1972a:18) notional categories and distinctions are probably influenced by a knowledge of the forms, and, as F.
Palmer pointed out (see above), semantic considerations may well be
used in arriving at formal categories. It is always possible, hypothetically, that a pedagogical grammar designed this way, according to teachers'
intuitions, along principled lines, should made a general contribution to
the study of language.

1.4. Grammar: the Psychological Dimension

1.4.1. Overview

If the radical dynamic view of a pedagogical grammar is adopted, then
some principled psychological basis must be found. Learning theory is
still very much in a state of ferment (cf. Thomson 1969:109), but two
broad fields may be distinguished, namely, behaviourist and cognitive
theory. The first field sees learning in mechanistic terms, as non-
conscious habit formation; the second sees it as involving both mechanical
responses and conscious processes in the mind.

Behaviourists including reinforcement and contiguity theorists reacted to
older traditional approaches because they were too speculative and
unscientific. As will be shown, they (Thorndike, Guthrie, Watson, Tolman,
Spence, Miller, Skinner, et al.) took a hard line towards considering
abstract mental processes although neo-behaviourists (Osgood, Mowrer)
have turned to what seems to be the beginnings of a compromise talking
of "mediation" between external stimuli and responses. The cognitive

approach, broadly speaking, may cover various schools including Gestalt psychology (Wertheimer, Koffka, Köhler, etc.), Piaget, Inhelder, Vygotsky and more recently Bruner, Gagné, Ausubel and others. What these all have in common is an interest in explaining the internal mental operations that the behaviourist wished to avoid.

It is outside the scope of the present work to give a detailed account of all the theories. A brief survey of behaviourism and its effect on language teaching, especially in the United States, will be given, and then a more specific approach will be adopted and outlined as being particularly appropriate to the construction of a pedagogical grammar as envisaged in the previous section. This will be orientated towards the conscious assimilation of the foreign language in line with cognitive methodology.

1.4.2. Behaviourism and Cognitive Psychology

Twenty years ago the situation might have seemd simple. There was a philosophy of language teaching held by specialists which reflected a neat match between linguistics and psychology, at least in the United States. Bloomfieldian linguistics was in accord with behaviouristic psychology and a reasonably coherent view was possible as to how to construct a pedagogical grammar. Perhaps the guiding principle that governed both behaviourist psychology and linguistics as conceived by the Bloomfieldian school was the strict reliance on data that were empirically verifiable. That is to say, no statements could be made on what was not directly, overtly observable. Thus nothing that was hypothetically supposed to occur in the human mind could be taken into account in a theory of learning unless it could be openly demonstrated. All speculation of a mentalist character was then excluded from "science". The immediate result of this was that findings from animal psychology--animals being more amenable to laboratory experiment--were extrapolated to cover human behaviour. This empirical scientific attitude did not cover the forming of hypotheses about what was not directly physically observable and then finding some empirical evidence for them. It was firmly based on the physically observable from the start. Learning was described behaviouristically and language "verbal behaviour", to use B.F. Skinner's term, distributionally without recourse to meaning and ideas which were regarded as a mentalist preoccupation have no place in scientific investigation. As Wilga Rivers reports, referring to Skinner's <u>Verbal Behavior</u> (1951):

> Any notion of "idea", Skinner says, is an explanatory fiction, in that we build into the "idea" all the properties needed to explain the behaviour. "The speaker is merely the <u>locus</u> of verbal behaviour, not a cause," and "knowing what one is saying" is on the same level as knowing anything else in the stimulating environment. Similarly "meaning" is a misleading concept, as it is traditionally understood. "We must find," says Skinner, "the functional relations which govern the verbal behaviour to be explained." In conformity with the tenets of strict behaviourism, Skinner tries to limit himself to the physically observable.

(Rivers 1964:25)

The overall approach to learning in the post-war period that was most widely accepted up until the late sixties was that of stimulus-response psychology. The most famous experiments wehre those conducted by the Soviet psychologist Pavlov where dogs were conditioned to salivate at the ticking of a metronome, which they associated with the arrival of food. The food always arrived after the metronome and there was no attempt to teach the dogs to act in any way in order to obtain the food. However, Pavlov's classical conditioning was not seen as being directly relevant to human learning by either Pavlov or his followers. Human beings were capable of a higher form of neural activity - abstraction through language (Rivers 1964:26). In stimulus-response psychology as developed by Watson, Skinner et al., human as well as animal behaviour was to be accounted for without resorting to abstraction in any non-mechanistic sense. All human learning came to be seen as a form of conditioning. Extrapolation from animal experiments was considered respectable. As Skinner put it, the advance in the analysis of behaviour allows a certain amount of optimism:

> Much of the experimental work responsible for this advance had been carried out on other species, but the results have proved to be surprisingly free of species restrictions. Recent work has shown that the methods can be extended to human behaviour without serious modification.
>
> (Skinner 1957:3)

So verbal behaviour, in Skinner's terms, was composed of conditioned responses. Unlike classical conditioning, however, the learner has to act in order for the appropriate learning to occur. The correct response is the one which is reinforced and consequently learned rather than those possible responses that might occur that are not reinforced. In other words, the action of the learner is instrumental in achieving the desired result. The reinforcement that he receives makes it possible for the relevant response to reoccur regularly and thus become a habit. The behaviouristic view of language is outlined by Skinner as follows:

> In all verbal behaviour under stimulus control there are three important events to be taken into account: a stimulus, a response, and a reinforcement. These are contingent upon each other, as we have seen, in the following way: the stimulus, acting prior to the emission of the response is likely to be reinforced. Under this contingency, through a process of operant discrimination, the stimulus becomes the occasion upon which the response is likely to be emitted.
>
> (Skinner 1957:81)

Skinner's rejection of any speculation as to how the human brain might organise incoming stimuli has been somewhat modified by neo-behaviourists such as Mowrer and Osgood, who allow for some kind of "mediating response" within the organism. While still allying themselves within the basic philosophy of behaviourism, neo-behaviourists leave the extreme position of not dealing with the observable and try to posit some kind of intermediary organisation between the observable response (see Rivers 1964: 33ff. and 182ff., Greene 1972:183, 193, Chastain 1971:66, etc.). However, the real challenge to the behaviourist account of language and language learning only came when Chomsky wrote his famous and virulent attack on Skinner's <u>Verbal Behavior</u> (Chomsky 1959).

The question now arises as to what a behaviouristic pedagogical grammar might look like. It is perhaps not worthwhile speculating on all the possible applications of behaviourist theory to the writing of grammars, even grammars for learners. The simplest thing to do is to take Bloomfield's position as expressed in <u>Language</u> (1933) as a guideline and see how it has been applied. Perhaps the key characteristic of Bloomfield's approach is the ambiguous position taken towards the expression of language meaning. He did not reject meaning as some claim. This is clear by the following statements:

> Accordingly we say that the speech-utterance trivial and unimportant in itself, is important because it has <u>meaning</u>: the meaning consists of the important things with which a speech utterance is connected, namely the practical events.
>
> (Bloomfield 1933:27)

> We can define the meaning of a speech form accurately when this meaning has to do with some matter of which we possess scientific knowledge. We can define the names of plants or animals by names of the technical terms of botany or zoology, but we have no precise way of defining... love or hate... and these latter are in the great majority.
>
> (Bloomfield 1933:27)

> The statement of meanings is therefore a weak point in language-study and will remain so until human knowledge advances very far beyond its present state. In practice, we define the meaning of a linguistic form...in terms of some other science.
>
> (Bloomfield 1933:27)

However, Bloomfield and his followers, faced with the difficulties connected with the description of meanings and the strict empirical requirements of behaviourist psychology, concentrated on describing the structure of language without much recourse to meaning. A pedagogical grammar on these lines would then be a simplified version of a distributional analysis of the elements of language in linear structure, which would provide a very natural input to structural drills, i.e. language patterns designed to be "overlearned" in a mechanical unthinking manner according to the dictates of Skinnerian psychology. Bloomfield once expressed caution (as Chomsky was to later) about the application of linguistics to the "control of human events" (Bloomfield 1933:509). However, inconsistently on his part, he later advocated the full scale application of structural linguistics along behaviourist lines (Bloomfield 1942, cf. also Currie 1973:34). His most eminent disciple, Charles Fries, produced <u>The Structure of English</u>, which Crystal has called "the most systematic application of the structuralist approach to language" (Crystal 1971:210). But as the title implies, it dealt only with language structure (see also 1.3.). Nevertheless, Fries showed an interest in the problem of meaning as he made quite clear in his article "Meaning and Linguistic Analysis" (1954).

> In general, for linguists, the "meanings" of an utterance consist of the correlation, regularly recurrent sames of the stimulus-situation features, and the regularly elicited sames of the response features.
>
> (Fries 1954, in Allen 1958:107)

Meanings were divided into different modes resulting in the threefold division of lexical, structural and socio-cultural meanings. In each case Fries speaks of the "automatic recognition" of "recurrent sames" and in a note he says:

> I take recognition here to mean not a conscious act of identification but rather an automatic conditioned response connecting the patterns of vocal sound with recurrent features of experience. Recognition is itself a "meaning" response. I am assuming that every kind of meaning has this kind of process.
>
> (Fries 1954, in Allen 1958:106)

A behaviouristic grammar might be adapted to different linguistic theories but the link between behaviourism and Bloomfieldian structuralism is so apparent that Bloomfieldian grammar would seem to offer the best illustration. And it would appear that a strict distributional account of structure with no attempt to find notional grounds for any part of the description would form the bulk of such a behaviouristically orientated presentation of language information. It is hard to see how statements on meaning could be incorporated into such a grammar due to this concentration on the importance of structure. It would be up to the textbook writer to develop materials for conditioning the relevant structures to their meaning, particularly in the form of pattern practice and dialogue memorisation. The structural patterns would thereby be established as habits. Paul Roberts who has produced three pedagogical grammars (mainly for native speakers, however) wrote one of them before he was influenced by transformational-generative theory, viz. Patterns of English (1956), which might give some indication of the type of grammar of the kind hypothesised here. For pedagogical reasons, he decided to simplify the terms and not follow Fries' labelling of form classes, etc. by numbers and letters. Instead, he cautiously reintroduced old terms like noun and verb but with appropriate warnings that they were not to be taken in the traditional manner. A grammar for foreign learners might in some way provide the necessary contexts (linguistic and socio-cultural) for the appropriate conditioning of form to meaning to take place. For the learner himself, the conscious recognition of form-meaning relationships was not usually seen as primary. Grammatical rules, however, might be expressed in a neat, easily understandable way for the learner in the form of a review after he has gone through the process of automisation through overlearning--the process by which he learns to respond immediately and without reflection to the appropriate stimuli. The possibility for the Bloomfieldian pedagogic grammar of organising form-meaning relationships is difficult to imagine. In fact, as long as such a grammar provides the basic structural facts in a relatively non-technical way, the rest might well be done by the materials writer and classroom teacher. For the behaviourists, teaching

> involved not the proper arrangement of information to be presented, but the establishment of learned connections between selected stimuli and appropriate reinforcement.
>
> (Chastain 1971:68)

There is perhaps one aspect of a grammar designed along behaviourist lines that might be supplied in order to turn it from a standard presentation of the facts of language into something more specialised and appropriate to potential use by teachers and materials writers, i.e. the contrastive aspect. In other words, a grammar specifically for learners of English as a foreign language (as opposed to one like Patterns of English) would be ordered to take into account the structure of the native language of the learners. It would therefore be designed to cope with the problem of transfer, that is, the effect of already learned tasks on the learning of new tasks, or, in present terms, the influence (positive and negative) of the native language on the acquisition of the target language. According to one's conception of how best to facilitate transfer, one will highlight certain parts of the learning task (the target language) over others.

Contiguity theorists like Guthrie were pessimistic about transfer, believing that the best way to teach something is to teach that specific thing and pay little attention to what has already been learned. However, reinforcement theorists such as Skinner had a more positive approach. The generally accepted principle was that transfer from one situation to another is roughly speaking proportional to the similarity between the two situations (cf. Craig 1966:46). It therefore follows that a behaviourist contrastive pedagogical grammar should highlight those areas of the target language that differ from the native language. These areas would be the "problem areas" and indicate to the teacher and textbook writer the proper emphases in teaching and constructing materials. However, the vast difficulty of comparing different languages puts considerable obstacles in the way of a behaviouristic contrastive grammar, since, strictly speaking, languages are observed by Bloomfieldians to be separate independent systems, and if we are not allowed to resort to mentalist notions to compare them, we may find it impossible to establish exactly what is "similar" and what is not. A further point is that writers of a behaviouristic contrastive grammar, if it were feasible, would have to adopt an explicit attitude towards the use of translation, should it be organised to facilitate translation exercises. Audio-lingualists are by and large against using overt comparisons between languages as, in their opinion, it would facilitate negative transfer, and in this they seem to follow Guthrie's strictures about the specificity of learning tasks. But theoretically there is no reason why a behaviouristic grammar should not provide language conversions, i.e. translations (for use at advanced levels perhaps) provided the basic problem of arriving at a method of establishing proper contrasts and similarities is resolved. A Chomskyan approach, positing universals and inate process in the human mind, would help to resolve this problem, but the premises of Chomsky's arguments are clearly inimicable to behaviouristic psychology. A contrastive or "transfer" grammar on behaviouristic lines depends on the linguist's prior establishment of comparison techniques. No linguistic theory with the same mechanistic premises as behaviourist psychology has really succeeded in solving the problem.

Lastly, the advisability of concentrating on problem areas has been criticised both by audio-lingualists who declare that the whole language system should be presented in a balanced manner since everything related to everything else, and also by those who question whether the superficially similar elements in the target and native languages are always more easily learned than dissimilar elements. Swedes may, for example, find Norwegian harder to learn well than German. Studies of language errors have revealed that there are other than linguistic reasons for the difficulty of given linguistic items to be learnt (cf. Corder 1967, Nickel 1971b). Moreover, recent studies have indicated that a positive use of the native language may help rather than hinder transfer. In conclusion behaviourist psychology and structural linguistics can only offer a structural description of the native and target languages with no clear indication how they should be related or if they should be related at all.

Looking back on the behaviourist approach to language teaching, it is now possible to say that, although it killed some old myths and underlined the importance of structured practice, it ultimately failed to achieve the successes it promised (Chastain 1971:77-8). Bloomfield's advice to teachers that all learning is overlearning is now seriously criticised. Both behaviourism itself and Bloomfieldian linguistics are seen as very limited approaches. There has been a revival of the cognitive mentalist tradition allowing for hypotheses about the internal processes of the mind. A. Keuleers, who has been experimenting with the effects of cognitive drills which demand conscious insight on the part of the learner and not mechanical responses, states that there have been three historical constants in teaching methodology (Keuleers 1974:2ff.), namely insight into rules and conscious application, the direct contextual approach and the functional skills method (e.g. the audio-lingual method). None of them alone have provided all the solutions and we must seek an integration of all three. He reports considerable success with his methods, used with university students. Research on the effectiveness of cognitive methods as reported in Chastain (1971:128-30) proves to be promising as well as that conducted in Gothenburg, Sweden, in the GUME project (Oskarsson 1972, 1974). Since modern cognitive theory includes many facets of behaviourism rather than offering an alternative "wonder method", and since the initial results of applications seem promising, it is this approach that is adopted in this work. Moreover, since a notional approach is favoured here, it is logical that a psychological theory that deals with internal mental processes is a more suitable candidate for dealing with the problem of meaning in pedagogical grammar than a theory that refuses to discuss meaning except in terms of conditioning. The overview has involved much overgeneralisation and in the last analysis the choice of cognitive theory has admittedly involved a certain amount of instinctive feeling. Learning theory is still in its infancy and apart from the promising signs in the research done so far, there is not much more to go on. However, enough has been written to formulate a systematic approach to the matter.

One of the most coherent and interesting approaches to cognitive psychology is that of Ausubel and this will form the basis of the analysis in the third chapter.

1.4.3. A Cognitive Approach

The design of a pedagogical grammar must obviously be conceived so as to make the learning task effective or, as Ausubel puts it, "the art and science of presenting ideas and information effectively--so that clear, stable and unambiguous meanings emerge and are retained over a long period of time as an organised body of knowledge--is one of the principle functions of pedagogy". The crucial underlying principle of the cognitive approach is to link new ideas and information to ideas and information that already exist in the learner's cognitive structure. New information must be anchored first to old information before becoming stable and capable of providing anchorage itself to subsequent new information. Anchoring typically involves "subsumption" of the correlative type (Ausubel 1968:100-1) whereby the new material extends, elaborates, modifies or qualifies previously learned propositions. If the learning material is presented to the learner in a sufficiently lucid manner and shown to be relevant, there is a good chance that learning will take place. New information need not, of course, be anchored to old in order for learning to take place. Ausubel distinguishes between meaningful learning (by subsumption) and rote learning which involves absorbing the material independently of what is already learned in an arbitrary and verbatim way. While meaningful learning is typical of the human mind, rote learning is shared by men and animals and is less interesting (despite the extrapolations of behaviourists) as far as the study of human learning is concerned. Summarising the cognitive view, Chastain says:

> ...cognitive theory maintains that the mind processes information to be learned. In order for this process to be maximally efficient, the material must be meaningful. The mind is not a computer. It does not simply absorb information in bits and pieces which it never forgets. The indications are that it organises the material into meaningful chunks which it relates to information already contained in the individual's cognitive structure. The material is then stored for future use. The fact that meaningful relationships enhance learning does not imply that rote learning is impossible, but that it is less efficient and less productive.
>
> (Chastain 1971:87)

Thus according to this view new information presented to the learner can be handled in three possible ways as represented in the following diagrams:

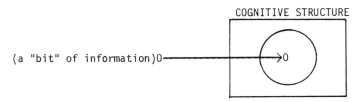

Fig. 3. New information accepted by learner and subsumed in a concept already existing in the cognitive structure (meaningful learning).

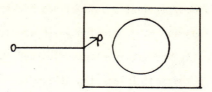

Fig. 4. New information accepted by learner and kept independent of concepts already learned (rote learning).

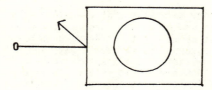

Fig. 5. New information not accepted by learner.

If the mind is presented as an organising mechanism and not just a recipient of external stimuli, this does not imply that the teacher's role is thereby diminished. The teacher and materials writer must also organise material to be presented to the learner to assist the natural processes of the mind, to lighten the task and reduce the learning time. To this end Ausubel proposes the technique of providing <u>organisers</u>. Organisers facilitate the meaningful learning of information by so arranging it that it relates clearly to old information. The learner may do this to some extent but not so efficiently as the pedagogue who a. knows the subject matter and b. is by definition sophisticated in learning matters. Organisers may be <u>comparative</u> in that they use concepts in cognitive structure that are similar, linking the new with the old and at the same time clarifying the differences to facilitate discrimination. Organisers may also, in the case of totally new material, be <u>expository</u> in which case the subsumption involves the indication of a superordinate concept under which the new information may be included. <u>Advance</u> organisers provide very general concepts at a high level of abstraction at the beginning of a teaching course. All organisers must obviously be <u>learnable</u> and <u>stated in familiar terms</u> (Ausubel 1968:149). Fig. 6 below illustrates the use of organisers:

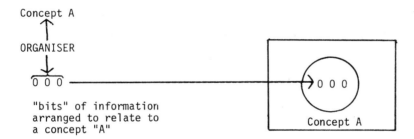

Fig. 6. New information organized by the pedagogue and accepted by the learner who already has concept A in his cognitive structure.

It seems to follow from this approach to the psychology of learning that a pedagogical grammar which organised the factual material--the systems and units of language--in terms of notions familiar to the learners and relating in a clearly relevant manner to previously learned information would provide an excellent method of learning. Distributional terminology, such as that used by Fries, could indeed be linked by organisers in some way to the learners' knowledge of mathematical and logical formulae, but how much more powerful would be an approach that exploited all the learner's experience of life including the meanings that are perceived through the medium of the native language. And if teaching material is to be organised along these lines, then surely pedagogical grammar in general should be arranged to make these notional organisers easy to extract from the language description. The superordinate concept of future reference itself could be an expository advance organiser to prepare for a more detailed elaboration of the different types of ways of referring to the future. These in turn could be organisers that would relate to the original advance organiser and enable the learner to compare and contrast similar concepts (types of future reference) already used through the medium of the native language. They would also serve as a base for the learning of the linguistic items and systems in the target language. This will be illustrated fully in the third chapter of this work.

Finally, if we accept that there is a need for a notional grammar, linking the new information incorporated in the grammar to concepts already in the learner's mind, we must also consider the problem in the light of the language information that already exists there, i.e. that native language. Not only the learner's knowledge of the world but also his inherent knowledge of his own language should be deliberately exploited. Translation as a learning strategy, as long as it does not involve the rote memorisation of rules (as in the grammar-translation method) may aid rather than hinder the learning process. Ausubel stresses that translation does not refer to the end product of teaching. Fluent speakers of a foreign language do not consciously translate from their native language. On the other hand, translation is a very good <u>mediating strategy</u> during the learning process. What is used in the learning phase does not have to be the terminal behaviour:

> In short, a cognitive process characterizing the acquisition of a new ability does not necessarily apply to the later exercise of that ability.
>
> (Ausubel 1968:70)

Later he states:

> Actually, it is both unrealistic and inefficient for the learner to try to circumvent the mediating role of his native language when learning a second language...

and

> ...numerous aspects of first language knowledge--the meaning of most concepts, the understanding of syntactical categories and functions, facility in using many structural patterns that are nearly identical in the two languages--are directly transferable to second-language learning. It would therefore be not only impracticable but also impossible not to make use of this knowledge in acquiring the second language.
>
> (Ausubel 1968:74)

From this we may conclude that a pedagogical grammar should facilitate the use of such mediating strategies by creating mediating devices between the two languages. The notional approach is particularly suited to establishing common ground between two languages, since we are not restricted by the problems of deciding about structural similarities without reference to semantic concepts. There is a much clearer case, then, for a contrastive pedagogical grammar if we adopt the cognitive approach. At the very least

a general pedagogical grammar should be so organised to facilitate the
use of intralanguage comparisons even if it is not specifically contrastive as between one particular language and another.

1.5. Grammar: the Social Dimension

1.5.1. The Problem

From what has been said in the preceding section, it may seem reasonable
to turn to Chomskyan grammar (i.e. generative syntax) for help in formalising the language information in the pedagogical grammar. The premises
of Chomskyan theory, being mentalist, stressing the organising mechanisms
of the human mind and accepting the feasability of language universals
(cf. Chomsky 1965 etc.), seem to fit neatly in with the basic philosophy
of cognitive psychology in general. However, experimentation with the
<u>formalisations</u> of grammar as conceived by Chomsky (e.g. transformational
rules) have not ultimately proved conclusive. Summing up her analytic account of this experimentation based on Chomsky 1965, Greene says:

> On both theoretical and experimental grounds it appears that the
> two-level concepts of deep and surface structure have psychological
> reality, although the operations for extracting "meaningful" deep
> structure from surface structure word order need not take the form
> of transformational rules. It is also argued that some form of
> deep structure representation is necessary to account for a speaker's
> ability to express "meanings" in sentence form. There is however
> much controversy as to whether underlying deep structure should be
> formulated as specified in transformational grammar or in the form
> of an even more abstract semantic representation.
>
> (Greene 1972:188; cf. also Marton 1972b)

Chomsky himself has wavered between what Greene calls his weak and strong
claim as regards the relationship between his model and the psychological
process of the mind:

> ...when Chomsky makes the stronger claim that he is describing
> the structure of cognitive processes, can he ignore the extreme
> complexity of the relation between speakers' linguistic knowledge
> and how it is actually put to use in the real world?
>
> (Greene 1972:196)

It is this extension of language description into what is here called the social dimension that has occupied linguists recently and which, as was discussed in 1.3., is of greater interest to language teachers and therefore of greater relevance to the radical conception of a pedagogical grammar. As early as 1968, McCawley became concerned with the interpretation of sentence meaning as being too limited in current theory:

> Disambiguation actually involves not merely linguistic competence
> but also the language user's factual knowledge; indeed it is
> merely a special case of the judgement of a speaker's intentions.
>
> (McCawley 1968:129)

And as has already been mentioned earlier, the school of generative semantics is currently concerned with trying to establish ways of formalising the social dimension as related to the interpretation of utterances, notably in the form of establishing the relevant <u>presuppositions</u>. (Cf. Garner 1971, Fillmore 1971, Stalnaker 1972, etc.) For example, Binnick in discussing the difference between <u>will</u> and <u>going to</u> says that <u>will</u> implies a causal relationship (see 2.2.2.), i.e. it is often elliptical assuming another clause or statement, e.g.:

   I will drown. (--if nobody helps me, for example)

In other words, there is a difference in presupposition (Binnick 1972: 3ff.).

Sociolinguists have also taken up the idea of extending the notion of competence (Chomsky 1965) into the social dimension. Hymes coined the term <u>communicative competence</u> (Hymes 1972) claiming that not only does the native speaker possess the ability to understand and produce syntactically well-formed utterances, but also utterances which are appropriate to the situation. A sentence, for example, can be well-formed in the first sense but ill-formed in the second sense, e.g.:

    ? I await your letter with impatience

instead of:

    I am looking forward to hearing from you

or more subtly:

    ? I write to tell you some news about your uncle

    (in a letter to a close friend) (see 2.2.5.)

Appropriacy is then explained convincingly as a part of competence. It therefore follows that it could be somehow accounted for in the grammar. Unfortunately, the present state of the art does not yet allow for a well-motivated set of formalisations and the subject is still in its infancy, with many conflicting interpretations according to whether the basic premises are seen as philosophical, linguistic or sociological (cf. Garner 1971). However, something has to be done, especially in the face of the learner's needs which are communicative in character. Jespersen himself saw this:

> The essence of language is human activity--activity on the part of one individual to make himself understood by another, and activity on the part of the other to understand what was in the mind of the first. These two individuals, the producer and the recipient of language, or as we may more conveniently call them, the speaker and the hearer, and their relations to one another,

should never be lost sight of, if we want to understand the nature of language and of that part of language which is dealt with in the grammar.

(Jespersen 1924, repr. 1965:17)

A basic framework will therefore be presented here to cope with the problem in the absence of any detailed coherent scheme devised by any one particular theorist competent to do so.

1.5.2. An Interim Solution

It seems necessary to adopt the distinction, a "convenient classification" as Cherry termed it (1971:243), that Charles Morris made between syntactics (signs and relations between signs), semantics (relations between signs and the designata) and pragmatics (aspects which involve sign users) (Morris 1964). The social dimension of language is related to the third semiotic category: pragmatics. As Cherry puts it:

...associations of signs and designata in the mind of someone, in some specific situation, are semantic-pragmatic questions.

(Cherry 1971:244)

Montague (1972) develops this idea of pragmatics, wishing to make it more precise, following on from Bar-Hillel who suggested that

...pragmatics concerns itself with what C.S. Peirce had in the last century called indexical expressions. An indexical word or sentence is one where the reference cannot be determined without knowledge of the context of use.

(Cherry 1971:142)

(Here pragmatics seems to refer rather more specifically to deixis.) Montague suggests that such notions as "truth" and "satisfaction" that have been used in connection with semantics should also be applied to pragmatics, only incorporating the context of use. Stalnaker (1972)

defines semantics as being basically concerned with the definition of truth conditions for the sentences of various languages, semantics being therefore the study of propositions:

> Generally the study of formal semantics has proceeded by first setting up a language, and then laying down rules for matching up the sentences of that language with propositions or truth values.
>
> (Stalnaker 1972:382)

Pragmatics, however, studies linguistic acts and the contexts in which they are performed. There are two problems, says Stalnaker, the first to define interesting types of speech acts and speech products and the second to characterise the features of the speech content which determine which proposition is expressed by a given sentence. The sort of speech acts to which he is referring are <u>assertions</u>, <u>commands</u>, <u>predictions</u>, <u>requests</u>, <u>promises</u>, etc. With regard to the notion of presupposition, <u>people</u> rather than <u>sentences</u> make presuppositions in pragmatics (<u>as opposed to semantics</u>). If, for example, we take a popular example such as the sentence:

It is rather hot in here, isn't it?

this may in certain definable contexts function as a request for permission to open the window or a command (ironically) for the hearer to shut the window. In another context it may be a request to the hearer to engage in spoken interchange, i.e. as "phatic communion", to use Malinowski's term. As far as semantics is concerned, we are interested only in establishing such information as the fact that there is a place and that this place is being called rather hot, all of which can be related to the basic meaning of the linguistic signs without reference to the specific context of use. As far as pragmatics is concerned, we are concerned with the speaker's intentions <u>in a particular communicative situation</u>.

The importance of separating pragmatics from semantics, however arbitrary it may on occasions seem, is that it gives us a means whereby we can specify basic meaning patterns independently of context and then in a second stage speak of usage, i.e. pragmatics. As will be shown in the following chapters, a great deal of unnecessary complexity and confusion has arisen over not consistently distinguishing these two stages of the interpretation of meanings. An important simplification can be achieved if a small number of semantic meanings explaining a given form (or set of forms) are isolated first and then, only later, discussed in relation to possible pragmatic meanings. It should be noted here, however, that we cannot make a strict division between semantic and pragmatic meaning in terms of knowledge of the real world. This would reduce semantics to a very unrestricted area. Pragmatics must be restricted here to that area which pertains to the knowledge of <u>particular situations</u>. It is then the study of the particular, where semantics is the study of the general. The pedagogical grammar will generally attempt to maximise the number of generalisations we can make and thereby minimise the number of pragmatic statements. Both semantics and pragmatics deal in some sense or other with the real world. If we were to find, for example, that

    Did John go home?

and all sentences structurally similar to it were <u>questions</u>, then we would state this in the semantic component as a generalisation irrespective of particular situational contexts. If we were to find, on the other hand, that this type of sentence could also commonly function as a statement or a promise, then its status as a question form would be a matter of pragmatics. Ultimately, the pedagogical grammarian will judge which solution is the most economic or informative, bringing in outside considerations. The semantic/pragmatic distinction should be seen as a heuristic device for the moment anyway and does not need to be faultless from a logical or philosophical point of view as long as it serves this purpose.

Furthermore, we may make a broad distinction between semantic and pragmatic presuppositions and implications in that the former are applicable in all or nearly all contexts, whereas the latter relate to particular situations. For example, the co-occurrence of the first person pronoun I (with an auxiliary denoting futurity and a main active verb denoting an action within the control of the agent) may be said to potentially entail the notion of intention. Thus:

    I will do the work for you

implies that "I" intend to do the work. Intention is then not part of the basic meaning of will but rather a general semantic implication that may obtain whenever certain semantic or syntactic conditions are fulfilled. It is to be noted that:

1. to cover the flexibility of language meaning we often have to speak of potential (as opposed to necessary) presuppositions and implications. Given the fulfilment of certain conditions, irrespective of the parti-

cular communicative goal of the speaker (warning, predicting, threatening, promising), the hearer must be aware that a certain presupposition or implication may obtain.

2. Once the description moves on to detailing conditions that must obtain in a <u>particular</u> situation, we have left the realm of semantics proper. The actual characterisation of the above example as a <u>promise</u> presupposes that the speaker is sincere at the time of the particular utterance, that he is in a position to do the work, and so on. This would therefore be a matter of pragmatic presupposition. Of course, not all presuppositions or implications are equally interesting or equally important from a pedagogical point of view. Some are esoteric and some are too obvious to be worth mentioning in the grammar.

For the pragmatic part of the grammar, a number of <u>speech acts</u> may be set up according to what is deemed to be pedagogically relevant. The formalisation of speech acts could follow the general lines set out by Austin (1962) as developed by McCawley (1968), Boyd and Thorne (1969), Ross (1970) and others. The first element contains the information that tells us what type of speech act it is (promising, requesting, etc.), and the second contains the proposition which may be interpreted (under the present system) independently by semantics and syntax (syntactics). Thus the sentence (although a speech act is not necessarily a "sentence"):

Where are the matches?

may be formalised as, for example:

I imp you you inform me: where are the matches.

or alternatively:

(PLEASE (INFORM ME)) where are the matches.

There are a large number of possible formalisations one might devise, and it is not necessary to stick closely to those of theoretical linguists who wish to incorporate their formalisations into a more general linguistic theory. Thus the general heading REQUEST or POLITE REQUEST is quite sufficient for a pedagogical pragmatic label. The formalisations need to conform to pedagogic theory, however, and the cognitive concepts of Ausubel are relevant here, particularly his idea of <u>perceptual</u> organisers which are built-in mechanical aids (both visual and oral) like underlining, capitalisation, etc. (Ausubel 1968:330ff.). It must all the same be made clear in the grammar that a speech act is a relation between the <u>speaker</u> and the <u>hearer</u> (or <u>writer</u> and <u>reader</u>), i.e., that the grammar is offering the learner information about how to use defined stretches of the target language to perform specified acts of communication, or how to grasp the <u>complete meaning</u> (cf. Strawson 1973) of such an utterance, i.e. the semantic <u>and</u> pragmatic meaning, when he hears or reads them. Whatever organiser is used, perceptual or otherwise, this fact must be given due importance. In a contrastive pedagogical grammar there would be a clear case for giving such pragmatic information as the characteristics of speech acts in the native language.

Identifying the types of speech acts necessary for a pedagogical grammar is not all that is required. Information must be given in some cases about the conditions that must obtain for a given utterance to be interpretable as a given speech act, the so-called happiness conditions (i.e. pragmatic presuppositions). Very often, however, all that is needed is a single word or expression like "threat" or "prediction" and the learner's experience of the world will be sufficient for him to know what normally constitutes a threat or prediction. Precise logical definitions are not necessary in such cases. Furthermore, the distinction made by Austin (1962) between <u>locutionary acts</u> and <u>perlocutionary acts</u>, the first involving the utterance itself as constituting the act (as in promises), the second relating to the result of the utterance (persuasion, etc.) may be collapsed: the term <u>performative</u> may cover both. Austin himself said that all utterances are to some extent performative (cf. also Warnock 1973) and for present purposes the "umbrella" term will do.

A further point that should be made is that the "pragmatic" and the "semantic" meanings may on occasion seem to come very close to each other, such that a given utterance with a given semantic meaning may have, or seem to have, a one-to-one relation with a pragmatic category, i.e., a given performative act, for example, inverted order "question" forms correlate closely with requests. Another example would be:

I will go to Prague this spring.

which might at face value seem to suggest a one-to-one relationship between the semantic notion of future reference, and the pragmatic, performative notion of prediction. However, this particular reference to the future might function as a threat or a promise as well as a simple prediction. It is true that a promise or a threat entails some idea of prediction, and it is easy to see that a philosophical argument could develop here as to the status of pragmatic versus semantic meaning. The admittedly leaky semantic/pragmatic opposition does, however, seem a useful distinction, at least as an interim solution to the problem in language pedagogy.

Finally, a pedagogical grammar should also provide information about general semantic presuppositions and implications where necessary as a prerequisite for the correct use of given items. The use of <u>will</u> in the above example involves a presupposition, whatever speech act is being made, namely, that it implies that the subject's going to Prague is contingent upon some other state or event. This particular presupposition may not always be very important but it is information that would be useful to the learner.

To conclude, a pedagogical grammar should provide basic information for the learner, teacher or textbook writer (all of whom may not be native speakers) about the syntax, the semantics and the pragmatics of the target language. The semantic and pragmatic parts of the description comprise its <u>notional</u> section. In the semantic component, the more generalised meanings, which are relatively independent of specific communicative situational factors, should be outlined including, where necessary, general presuppositions. Finally, the pragmatic component should provide a selection from all the possible speech acts realisable in the target language and, where necessary, their various pragmatic presuppositions and implications. These speech acts will be chosen for their pedagogic potential, and they will be formalised in a maximally informative way, given the defined aims of the particular grammar in question. In each case, the speech act should contain two components, the <u>performative</u> and the <u>propositional</u> (cf. Sharwood Smith 1972). It should be made clear that the performative component is an act of communication between a speaker and a hearer. Evidently, a large part of the burden of relating language to context must be shouldered by the teacher and the textbook. A pedagogical grammar that did all this by itself would be unrealistically large. However, it should be designed so that the social dimension of language can be related to its forms, especially where dictionaries do not provide help, i.e. where it is not just a case of single lexical items or idioms. Existing pedagogical grammars do, of course, contain semantic and pragmatic information. The chapter on focus, theme and emphasis in Quirk et al. (1973) is a good example of a principled approach to the problem. But the information given in grammars is not always related to any broad underlying principle. In this thesis, one possible approach is proposed in which an attempt is made to integrate certain favoured psychological, sociological and linguistic-philosophical concepts and techniques. This goal may seem overambitious, but it is a solution that needs to be tried, now that there are so many potentially useful ideas available in these different fields of enquiry.

CHAPTER TWO

2.0. FUTURE REFERENCE PAST AND PRESENT

2.1. An Overview

The framework adopted for this particular thesis entails the concept of future reference. The term reference or time reference should be understood as synonymous with time. This concept, which is justified on extralinguistic grounds, conflicts in certain respects with formal categories arrived at via linguistics, notably tense. That there is some correspondence between the formal category "tense" and the extralinguistic notion of time reference is obvious in that many categories of tense are given time labels, e.g. present tense, past tense, future tense, etc. Also, aspect is related to time, giving us categories such as present perfect or past progressive. That time and tense need to be distinguished has been widely recognised and it is now a standard view that English has in fact only two tenses: past and present (or past and non-past). Will and shall, which were traditionally related to the English future tense, are now usually grouped with the modal auxiliaries on formal grounds. On the other hand, the term tense is sometimes used confusingly as a semantic category indicating time reference. The following selection of quotations may serve to illustrate the rather confusing picture that may result from a cursory reading of twentieth century grammarians and "pedagogues":

Poutsma:(1928:218 and 206):

> The future tense is formed by means of the auxiliaries shall and will, which in narrating past events are changed into should and would.

and: (The future tense consists in)...the verb groups which are employed in describing an action or state subsequent to the primary dividing point.

Jespersen:(1909, repr. 1961:199):

I think it may be conceded that English has no real "future tense".

Kruisinga:(1925:47):

The future tenses are formed with the auxiliaries shall and will.

and: Other forms to express future time may also be considered as future tenses because the verb with which they are formed is entirely meaningless or at least quite subordinate in maaning to the infinitive or the verb in full meaning...to be, to be going to, to be about...

F. Palmer:(1965:2):

We shall not be referring to future tense at all in spite of having past and present tenses.

Jacobs and Rosenbaum:(1968:121):

Thus, when we are speaking about syntactic tense, we are speaking about a purely syntactic phenomenon, the alteration of the actual form of a word. Of course syntactic tense does have some semantic significance; it does have meaning, but this meaning is not directly correlated with time.

Seuren:(1969:148):

We shall, tentatively, simply envisage five operators of tense: Present(Pres), Past, Future (Fut), Perfect (Perf) and the universal tense (U). ...the simplest description of tense qualifiers is given by ascribing to them a semantic property of being placed in time...

McCawley:(1971:112):

The future tense in English differs mainly morphologically from the present and past. Its marker is morphologically a modal verb rather than an affix.

Quirk et al.:(1972:84):

English has two tenses: PRESENT TENSE and PAST TENSE.

Tredidgo:(1974:106):

Does English possess a future tense? Most teachers are convinced that it does, but most linguists doubt it, as did Jesperson... to argue

> that English has only two tenses (past and present) seems to me to be using the word tense in a highly restricted sense which may be useful in certain systems of linguistic analysis but which, except in teaching the sequence of tenses, is quite useless for language purposes.

The last writer indicates the main problem that concerns pedagogical grammarians and teachers. That is, that English seemingly has two tenses, with no future tense, and yet is perfectly capable of providing the speaker with means to talk about future time, with which tense is allegedly bound up. It is perhaps best to regard <u>tense</u> as a formal syntactic verbal category, following Jacobs and Rosenbaum, Palmer, Quirk and others, and leave the term <u>time reference</u> (or <u>time</u>) for the semantics of verbal forms. In teaching a language, however, we cannot keep to the safety of syntax. We have to teach meaning, and we have to come to grips with the problem of the semantic categories relating to time reference. It is necessary to provide the learner with the means of referring to the different time dimensions as well as teach him the more sophisticated notional aspects of time reference available in the target language which may or may not be available in the native language. If then we approach the problem from the semantic angle and ask what the meanings of the English verb are with respect to future reference, we arrive at a number of forms with different syntactic behaviour. <u>Will</u>, <u>shall</u> and <u>'ll</u> occupy the major place in the literature. But the following forms must also be included:

1. <u>going to</u>
2. <u>be to</u>
3. Composite forms beginning with <u>will</u> or <u>shall</u>, e.g. <u>will have been</u>

4. Forms related to the present tenses (simple and progressive).

It will be seen that future states and events being inherently uncertain may be referred to with many different shades of meaning ranging over the notions of certainty, arrangement, possibility, probability, volition, intention, urgency, necessity, doubt and command to the name the more common ones. Because the future state or event is in the future it may be viewed in an extremely large number of ways and any account of these meanings has first to try and isolate these meanings and then to find some powerful generalisations which will fit the meanings into some kind of system. It has to be said that more attention seems to have been paid to the isolation and listing of meanings than to devising systems that will simplify the picture. The language teacher, however, urgently needs the simplifications and the modal descriptions devised by people such as Joos, Ehrman, Diver and others need too much pedagogic treatment for this purpose. The system to be described in the next chapter begins with the pedagogic aim in mind and perhaps this is the best way. However, it is best to first survey some of the treatments of future reference to date so that the typical problems may be illustrated and the next chapter set in a more general perspective. To do this the standard method of listing meanings will have to be followed. The inherent lack of system will be apparent especially in the earlier grammarians.

2.2.   General Survey

2.2.1. Will and Shall (Including Composite Forms)

These two forms are now regarded as modal auxiliaries (cf. Strang, Thorne, etc.), syntactically speaking, as they behave syntactically like the other forms in that group (may, must, should, etc.), though not everyone lists them as modals (cf. Fries 1940) or modals all the time (Thorne). One fundamental controversy that has existed for many years is the distribution of will and shall in the traditional paradigm: I shall, you will, etc. The main dispute concentrates on first person usage in particular. So in the "future tense" of English, as it used to be called, there is a division between the colourless future and another marked version supposedly expressing determination, promise, command, etc. This was the prescribed usage necessary for "good" English. The two paradigms run as follows:

Colourless Future

("plain", "neutral", "pure", etc.)

I shall   we shall
you will   you will
he will, etc.   they will

Marked Future

("modal", "volitional", etc.)

I will   we will
you shall   you shall
he shall, etc.   they shall

The distinction may be illustrated by the story of the man who was drowning and cried: "I will drown and no one shall save me." using the marked future in both cases and indicating his intention to drown and his refusal to accept help. Apart from the unlikelihood of such an interpretation given the situational context, it is highly doubtful whether it really illustrates the facts of modern English in the first place. In the Newcastle survey of English usage there was an overall acceptance of 50% for the sentence "I will be 21 tomorrow", which under the traditional scheme would be impossible since no one can intend (using a marked future) to be a certain age axcept in very bizarre circumstances (Mittins et al. 1970). Moreover, the survey showed significantly that examiners were amongst the most prescriptive group, not accepting the sentence. Moreover, it also provided proof that American usage (using mostly will) and British usage are not so far apart in this area as some would like to assert. The controversy is ably dealt with by Jespersen (1924) and Fries (1940) who give an account of this extremely complex semantic puzzle as it grew up from the rationalist analyses of grammarians like Lowth and Ward at the end of the eighteenth century and came into the discussion in textbook grammars in the first quarter of the nineteenth century. Fries analysed some twenty thousand instances in British and American dramas during the last 350 years and found that will with the first person has always been used more than shall (70-90%) in independent declarative sentences, that will now seems to be used throughout the paradigm rather than shall, especially in American English. The only place where shall is regularly found is in the first person in questions. Although this does not say much about the meaning, or about conversational usage, it would seem that these distributional facts alone referring to a possibly more stylised literary usage should give us cause to doubt the traditional picture.

Poutsma (1928) lists will and shall amongst the verbs denoting certainty and uncertainty and treats them in one place as modals and in another as markers of the future (apologising for the arbitrariness of the distinction). As markers of the future he analyses them within the framework of the categories: reported speech and non-reported speech, declarative sentences and questions. Future will is placed traditionally in the second and third persons in non-reported declaratives and questions. As throughout Poutsma the picture is clouded by frequent references to archaic English. Modal will in all persons can express "qualified conviction" as in: "Father will have come back." Poutsma also doubts whether will may occur as a simple future (colourless) in the first person ascribing such usage to "dialects" and non-British usage. Quotations are taken from Thackeray and Hardy (for example) (see Poutsma 1928, vol. 2, part 2:225ff.). Shall accordingly occurs regularly in the first person in non-reported declaratives and also in questions, for example, when the hearer's opinion is appealed to (Shall I take mine ease in mine inn). This allegedly is not a modal use. Modal shall is volitional, as in Shall I open the door?. Shall occurring in other persons is seen to be regarded by "the present generation" (Poutsma 1928:242) as only marked, being tinged with various notions which disqualify it as pure future. It is difficult to see how the shall of opinion (see above) is not also tinged with additional meaning. Poutsma does not do much more than list as many meanings of will and shall as he can, including archaic usage, and fails to present any clear simplifications.

Jespersen, reviewing the controversy (1961:290ff.), found no reason to use the traditional paradigms and discussed the reasons for the controversy as arising from the inherent uncertainty of future time. The future may be dependent or independent of human will; the will involved may be that of the speaker or the hearer; the subject of the sentence may be animate or inanimate; questions and statements pose different problems (questions sometimes anticipating the answer) and there is the general influence of emotions on the forms used (determination, diffidence, modesty, etc.). Jespersen also sees the problems as arising from the range of meanings of will and shall, i.e. the fact that they are required to perform too many semantic functions. Furthermore, he says that the old meanings of will and shall have not been entirely lost:

> Neither shall nor will has everywhere and in every combination lost the original meaning of obligation and volition, respectively.
>
> (Jespersen 1961:290)

Apart from one general rule, namely that will as a future auxiliary may be used everywhere except in those cases in which it might be misunderstood as implying volition (p. 297), Jespersen, like Poutsma, devotes a considerable amount of space to listing the modal and futuric meanings of these two forms. Thirty pages are devoted to will alone, and there are many interesting examples which would have had to be taken into account in a simplifying framework had Jespersen provided one. Below are some examples of the notions and forms illustrated in the grammar:

WILL

Volition, power, habit:	What is to be broke will be broke (inexorable fate)
	This hall will seat 500 (power, capacity)
	Women are generous--they will give you what they can (habit-consequence of willingness)
Non-futuric volition:	Boys will be boys (obstinacy)
	Who will have some lemonade?
Volitional future:	I will see him
Supposition:	The horses will be restless (cf. You will have heard.) (Past reference)
Other volitional uses:	I will do that (volition + certainty)
	You will have everything packed (command)
	If you will be so kind (in conditionals)

SHALL

Obligation:	No nobler pile of granite shall be found upon Dartmoor (predestination, no human will)
	You shall give the whole truth (volitional obligation)
Questions:	Shall I...? (asking for advice, etc.)
	Shall we...? (invitation)
Pure future:	I shall be sorry, prophetic biblical shall

This small selection of examples may serve to show how forbidding the task of simplification is. Jespersen ends up with a more complex version of the traditional paradigm whereby each person is matched against four categories of future: volitional, obligation, pure and "ambiguous". Under the first person singular, for example, we find that will is volitional or ambiguous and shall is pure. The volitional will occurs in an if-clause. The same analysis is applied to question forms. Elsewhere in the notional survey, Jespersen discusses his time divisions where A, B and C stand for the past, present and future respectively. Here we get the notions: Simple Future Time (C) where will and shall are grouped along with going to and the present tenses, Before-Future (Ca) including shall have and will have, and After-Future (Cc) where will and will have also occur (The sun will have set, for example). It would seem to the present writer that Jespersen here provided the seeds of a very useful presentation of future reference although the possibilities are not exploited, and, as has been mentioned earlier, Jespersen by and large concentrates on starting from the outer form and on listing the meanings along with a proliferation of notional labels.

Kruisinga (1925) provided a semantic framework using the old concept of tense, speaking, in the plural, of the future tenses. This had nothing to do with going to, etc. but referred to the way the time dimension is split up. Thus he makes three divisions (p. 47) into the Present Future (the action or state is thought of as a future from the point of view of present time), the Perfect Future (the action or state thought of as complete at a future time) and the Modal Future (the Present Future as used modally). This is supposed to cover the uses of shall and will (and their syntactic past forms). Kruisinga later introduces what he calls the Past Future tenses, i.e. the Preterite and Pluperfect Future tenses. These, he declares, are always used modally (apart from their use in reported speech). The past future is usually found in head clauses of hypothetical statements (I should have preferred, for example). One of the serious objections to be made here is that he never really brought in going to and the other future reference forms into his semantic framework. His main task was simply to account for the forms associated with will and shall. The semantic/syntactic distinction then continues to be blurred as regards time and tense, and will and shall linger on as the English future tense of old.

All efforts subsequent to Jespersen et al. have been devoted to bringing more order into the analysis of English verbs. Will and shall as auxiliaries with modal and futuric meaning have been analysed as part of the auxiliary system. Palmer provides the most obvious example (in Palmer 1965) of an attempt to put order into the traditional presentation. Other more radical attempts have been made to cope with systematising, e.g. Ota (1963), Diver (1964), Joos (1964) and Ehrman (1966) (cf. Kakietek's criticism in Kakietek 1970b). Twaddell provides a short concise account of form and meanings. Boyd and Thorne (1969) provide an interpretation within the general area of transformational grammar using the concept of illocutionary force, and there has been some discussion of will

(will-deletion) by TG grammarians, cf. Lakoff (1970), Binnick (1972) and Jenkins (1972). Leech, who dealt with time and modality on a very theoretical level, produced a book (Leech 1971) on meaning and the English verb, which contains a chapter devoted to future time and is probably the description which is the most suitable to a pedagogic application of all of them (see Keuleers 1974, for example). His description of will and shall is in some respects a development of Palmer's account. Both Palmer and (especially) Leech treat will and shall together with the other verbal forms of future reference. Finally, no account of the future with pedagogical aims in mind should ignore R.A. Close who has made a special study of this area (Close 1962, 1970, 1970b) with the language learner in mind. His account and exercises do not differ markedly from Palmer or Leech (cf. Close 1962, 1970a, 1970b).

Since a proper discussion of all accounts, many of which differ considerably from each other, would have to be fairly lengthy and go outside the scope of the present work, only those which are important and also directly relevant to the analysis to be presented later will be dealt with here.

Ehrman's treatment of the modal verbs merits attention (with regard to will and shall in particular) because it introduces the idea of basic meaning, thus promoting the cause of simplification, which makes it pedagogically attractive. The basic meaning of a modal is defined thus:

> ...the most general meaning of the modal in question, the meaning that applies to all its occurrences.
>
> (Ehrman 1966:10)

The meaning of the given modal may differ in its <u>overtones</u> which are derived from the basic meaning but add something of their own. For <u>will</u> and <u>shall</u> only, Ehrman has a special category called <u>time function</u> which relates to the effect of the surrounding context in the discourse on the temporal meaning of the modal in question (though inconsistently she does also use it for <u>should</u>, <u>ought</u> and <u>may</u>, cf. Kakietek 1970c:115). More specifically it is:

> ...a contextually conditioned variation in temporal relationship to the surrounding discourse which effects all overtones and basic meanings.
>
> (Ehrman 1966:11)

This must not be confused with the more general category of <u>temporal function</u> which indicates the time of any modal as related to the time of the utterance.

<u>Will</u> has the basic meaning of guaranteeing the occurrence of the predication. Thus in:

<u>The house will fall down</u>

the speaker guarantees that the falling down of the house will occur. If, however, the context imposes a <u>time neutral</u> interpretation (cf. time function), the occurrence may not uniquely refer to the future or to any time dimension as in the much discussed case:

<u>Oil will float on water</u>

The floating on water of the oil is simply guaranteed. The previous example has a <u>time future</u> interpretation (cf. time function) due to the context. <u>Will</u> has two overtones: <u>sequential</u> (cause-and-effect, logical sequence) and volitional (ranging from weak volition to command). An example of sequential will would be:

> The smaller the particle the further it will travel downwind

The following sentence would be an illustration of both volitional and sequential overtones respectively:

> If you won't eat it, then no one will (see also Ehrman:163)

One is tempted here to say that the last will in fact possesses both overtones since it is so obviously related to:

> No one will eat it (i.e. no one will want to eat it)

as well as:

> No one will eat it (i.e. I predict that no one will eat it)

and the sequential meaning as well.

According to Ehrman, the majority of occurrences of will have no element of volition. Those occurrences that do are predominantly time-neutral. Thus she would disagree, like Diver, Kakietek and others, that we should attribute volition to inanimate objects as Jespersen says is possible in examples like:

> Accidents will happen
>
> This hall will seat 550

Volition involves the subject being one of the guarantors of the predication. An example of this would be:

> He will fool around (i.e. he habitually insists or persists...)

And an example showing strong volition, best illustrated when the speaker and the subject are the same, would be:

<u>I will be firm: I will not give in</u>

In many examples one wonders how much of the meaning resides in the lexical meanings of the verbs and other words in the context. One feels that Jespersen intuitively may be right in associating the "accidents" example with volitional examples with animate subjects even though there is an illogicality involved. On the other hand, the idea of habitual occurrence with persistence, often implying a marked emotional reaction from the speaker, is a common factor in both animate and inanimate examples. Jespersen's comments are not to be taken as naive but rather as an acknowledgement of the illogical metaphorical aspects of language use. That we cannot say:

*<u>Accidents will happen unless they are told to stay away</u>

may as much be the consequence of overstretching a quasi-metaphor, as of proving that <u>will</u> must have here an entirely different meaning to the volitional <u>will</u>. Of course, this does not improve the general situation and in defence of Ehrman et al. we may say that any coherent system that clarifies the picture in a reasonably acceptable way is to be preferred to a subtler and more complex (and less analytic) discussion, at least for the purposes of language learning. Certainly Ehrman's concept of basic meaning is most useful, the main doubts arising inevitably from a specification of overtones and time reference. (The analysis presented later is different from Ehrman's but shares with it the idea of basic meaning, and the idea of meaning being conditioned by the context.)

<u>Shall</u> does not occur very often in Ehrman's American corpus. It has the

same basic meaning as will and is a "stylistic literary version of will (p. 56). It is usually a strong guarantee of the predication and seldom has volitional overtones.

Another contribution to the simplification of the shall/will problem was made by Boyd and Thorne (1969) in their performative analysis of modal verbs. Kakietek in his discussion of the matter (1970a) adopts their analysis for two important reasons:

> ...first it is by far simpler than that professed by traditional grammarians; second, it has the virtue of being capable of offering an exhaustive and uniform account of the two forms in all their possible contexts.
>
> (Kakietek 1970a:57)

Will and shall are analysed as markers of prediction. More accurately, they signal the fact that the speaker is performing a speech act of prediction. The illocutionary force of the sentence with will or shall may be formalised by an underlying performative: I predict. Thus

John will arrive on Thursday

may be interpreted as:

I PREDICT: John arrive on Thursday

and:

Oil will float on water

as: I PREDICT: Oil float on water

Note that prediction is not the same as futurity since the last example clearly refers to all time dimensions (i.e. time neutral according to Ehrman). This example may also be related to:

Oil floats on water

which although it may not be a paraphrase (though Kakietek refers to it as such, despite acknowledgement of the meaning distinction) carries basically the same meaning, the distinction residing in the illocutionary force: the version with will is a prediction; the other version is a statement. Shall in:

He shall go (i.e. the marked use of shall)

is analysed as having the illocutionary force of a guarantee and is represented in the underlying structure using the symbol imp:

I imp of myself He go non-past

Boyd and Thorne do not go into great detail analysing the various shades of meaning resulting in the uses of will and shall except by showing in a number of cases how everything can be reduced ultimately to the idea of prediction. (Kakietek 1969 and 1970c actually chooses a componential analysis by John Anderson as being more precise and formally based.) A preliminary treatment of verbal forms of future reference, owing much to Boyd and Thorne, was made by the writer in Sharwood Smith 1972, and contrastively in Sharwood Smith 1975.

Leech (1971) in certain respects continues the tradition of Jespersen as systematised by Palmer (in Palmer 1965). However, whereas Palmer is particularly interested in giving a formal account based on the syntactic facts of English, Leech's book is more interested in the meanings themselves (the syntactic spadework having been done by Palmer and others.). Leech, like Poutsma and many after him, notes that will and shall have a double function--as modal auxiliaries and as "auxiliaries of the future" (Leech 1971:52), remarking like the others that the two are intermingled and not always easy to distinguish. With regard to the future, he makes the following statement, which is reminiscent both of Ehrman's basic meaning and Boyd and Thorne's speech act:

> The word which most usefully characterises the future meaning of will and shall is PREDICTION--something involving the speakers/ judgement.
>
> (Leech 1971:52)
>
> The will/shall future is used in a wide range of contexts in which it is appropriate to make predictions.
>
> (Leech 1971:53)

Leech places these two forms at the head of a list giving the order of importance for the various forms used in future reference, i.e. will/shall, going to, Present Progressive, will/shall + -ing, Simple Present (p. 64). No motivation is given for this ordering. He also groups the same forms into three, in terms of degree of certainty. All forms using will and shall are grouped together in the second place. Again Leech does not comment on his motivation (perhaps because he feels no need to in view of his intended readers, i.e. foreign learners of English) (see 2.2.2.). As regards distribution in the paradigm, Leech says that futuric will may occur in all persons, but shall only in the first person. There is no comment about question forms. Furthermore, Leech refers to the possibility of using an "imaginary time-scale" (Leech 1971:53-4) where we refer to a later part of a book or article as in:

This will be presented in the next chapter

This will be called the Future Tense

In Ehrman's terms, this is the context giving (the modal) will a time-future interpretation (cf. the discussion in Ehrman 1966:34).

With regard to this modal <u>will</u>, Leech lists four possible meanings: <u>willingness</u>, <u>insistence</u>, <u>intention</u> and <u>predictability</u> (sic!). The first three may be called volitional--<u>weak</u>, <u>strong</u> and <u>intermediate</u> respectively. These may be illustrated as follows:

<u>Who will lend me a cigarette</u> ("weak volition")

<u>I will go to the dance and no one shall stop me!</u> ("strong volition")

<u>I will write tomorrow</u> ("intermediate volition")

Interestingly enough, Leech would allow

<u>My car will keep breaking down</u> (? strong volition)

as a personification of <u>car</u>, thus allowing for a metaphorical use of English.

The meaning of the fourth modal, confusingly called "predictability", may be illustrated thus:

<u>By now he will be eating dinner</u>

<u>That will be the milkman</u>

<u>Accidents will happen</u>

<u>Oil will float on water</u>

<u>This hall will seat 500</u>

<u>By now he will have arrived</u>

Leech admits that it is "only a small step" from here to the futuric <u>will</u> but does not support his distinction except with relation to an uncommon use <u>shall</u>. Generally, he accepts the useful generalisations that were made by Boyd and Thorne and by Ehrman. The delicacy of his distinction here nevertheless seems to suggest the more drastic generalisation (as made in Sharwood Smith 1972) of dismissing the modal-futuric opposition as a meaningful distinction (see 2.2.2.).

Shall in its modal meanings may only be volitional in the three senses mentioned above:

You shall stay with us as long as you like (weak volition--only in the second and third persons)

No one shall stop me (strong volition--only in the second and third persons)

I shall write tomorrow (intermediate volition--only with the first persons)

The predictability interpretation on a parallel with will is not possible. Also on strong and weak volition, Leech points out that shall implicates the will of the speaker rather than the subject--unlike will. In question forms, Leech has to introduce the idea of neutral volition (nearest to but a little less forceful than intermediate volition) to account for the meaning of shall in such examples as:

Shall I do your shopping for you?

In negative statements shall is not possible in the third intermediate sense of volition.

Lastly, Leech points out that the will/shall + -ing construction, apart from the standard progressive meaning of a temporary situation, can have an independent meaning, namely the "FUTURE-AS-A-MATTER-OF-COURSE" (Leech 1971:62ff.). Examples are:

The train will be arriving at midnight

I shall be writing to you soon

The event is viewed in its entirety and not within a temporal frame as for

the standard progressive meaning. Leech says that this construction
provides the speaker with the means of making a statement without any
possibility of volitional colouring. Compare the following two examples:

<u>I'll leave you tonight</u> (I've made up my mind)

<u>I'll be leaving you tonight</u> (as a matter of course)

The second statement places the possibility of a reversal in the
situation in the realms of the highly unlikely. (This meaning is not
independent of the general system to be outlined in the next chapter,
however.)

Leech makes a good number of valid and informative statements about the
meanings of <u>will</u> and <u>shall</u>, and he presents them within a coherent framework, which though not the one to be adopted, provides a much better base
for the construction of materials than Jespersen, who nevertheless is
equally informative. But even Leech's volitional distinctions may be
simplified (see next chapter).

Finally, the illuminating article "Predictive Statements" (McIntosh 1965)
should be mentioned particularly with regard to the "contingent" character
of <u>will</u> as opposed to <u>going to</u>. McIntosh points out that <u>will</u> often
signals events and states which are understood to be contingent on some
other state or event. Thus

<u>I will be sick</u>

carries with it an inference that the event is dependent on something else
in a way that the following sentence does not:

I am going to be sick

Thus we can imagine a wider context to illustrate the difference:

I will be sick if I go on eating this revolting soup

I am going to be sick and there is nothing I can do to stop it

It is not surprising that will seems particularly natural in the first person (in place of shall) when an if-clause follows.

2.2.2. Going to

Going to is called by Poutsma one of the further expedients to express futurity. He lists the following meanings: getting ready, purposing, an action or state in the course of preparation (Poutsma 1928 vol. 2: 244-5), outspoken intention, imminence (vol. 1:81). Jespersen says much the same, and both qualify their description of the meaning as implying imminent action by quoting a counterexample. Palmer notes that the form is very common in ordinary conversation, perhaps more common than will or shall (Palmer 1965:63). This is probably why Close devotes so much space to it in contrast with earlier textbooks which still had a "will/shall fixation". He lists it as relating to "present indications of what the future might bring" (Close 1970a:19-22) and to intention, though not uniquely so. With reservations conforming to McIntosh's comment mentioned above, Close considers going to as a plain future which can frequently replace will and shall. He also points out that, unlike will and shall, it can be used in if-clauses without the idea of volition. Note, however, that the use of going to actually alters the whole meaning of the if-clause. If becomes virtually synonymous with since:

<u>If you are going to leave at ten, you might as well take the bus</u>
This fits in with McIntosh's non-contingent interpretation of <u>going to</u>. Leech (1971) actually says that <u>going to</u> is inappropriate in most future conditional sentences, but in his examples he shows that he is thinking of <u>going to</u> in the main clause, e.g.:

+<u>If you accept that job, you are never going to regret it</u>

(cf. McIntosh's analysis). The exception to this rule, says Leech, is where the present circumstances are mentioned in the <u>if</u>-clause:

<u>We are going to find ourselves in difficulty if we carry on like this</u>

Leech makes a distinction between the future fulfilment of present intention and the future fulfilment of present cause as in the following two examples respectively:

<u>I am going to leave today</u>

<u>I am going to have a baby</u> (i.e. I am already pregnant)

Perhaps this distinction is not a vital one, residing mainly in the situational or linguistic context (and the lexical meaning of the main verb). The intention of the relevant agent is in a sense a "present cause". In Sharwood-Smith 1972 it was pointed out that the popular meaning of intention ascribed to <u>going to</u> is unmotivated precisely because intentionality is a meaning accrued from the context. There is not real reason to complicate the picture by distinguishing

<u>I am going to leave Edinburgh</u>

from

<u>It is going to rain</u>

since the association of <u>I</u> (human, animate agent, the speaker) and leave (action under the control of the agent or potentially so) with the basic meaning of going to (prediction on the basis of present circumstances) naturally implies intention. I, the speaker, am not likely to predict such an action of myself unless I have somehow made a decision about it. This is a question of pragmatics rather than basic semantic meaning in the verbal.

2.2.3. Be to

Poutsma treats be to as an occasional variant of will and shall, as in:

> The building is to be seven stories high

(Poutsma 1928:vol. 2:247)

This quite ignores the idea of plan or arrangement. However, elsewhere (vol. 1:49) he does say that the form can indicate arrangement or appointment as in:

> She is to be married next week

or a "dispensation of Providence" as in:

> ...the day which was to decide the fate of India...

The above examples have such a well-defined context that the meanings would be the same even if another form were used, e.g.:

> She will be married next week

Poutsma also says that be to serves to mark futurity where shall and will are not available, for example, giving English a "future infinitive" as in "effects to be wrought". The same remarks are made by both Jespersen (1961:354-5) and Kruisinga (1925:53) and Palmer who, like the others, notes its frequent use in the past (as in the third example above)

(Palmer 1965:142-3) and its other modal meaning of obligation, close to that of must or ought. Leech and Close follow the same line except that they both remark that it is rather the present tense meaning of the future (see 2.2.4.) than the will/shall future that be to relates to in its futuric sense. In other words, it has the meaning of a prearranged future. This, plus its syntactic characteristics, makes it a useful means of making abbreviated future statements as in newspaper headlines (cf. Close 1962:26 and Leech 1971:98). For example:

QUEEN TO LAUNCH NEW LINER!

This preplanned sense of be to seems to be the dominant characteristic of be to.

2.2.4. The Present Tenses

The use of the present tense in many languages other than English for the purposes of future reference may easily be attested. For example:

Piotr idzie jutro do szkoły	(Polish)
Pierre va demain à l'école	(French)
Peter geht morgen zur Schule	(German)
Peter gar till skolar i morgon	(Swedish)
Pieter gaat morgen naar school	(Dutch)
Pedro va mañana a la escuela	(Spanish)
Pëtr idët zavtra v školu	(Russian)
Petr dže jutře do šule	(Upper Sorbian)
Cras Petrus in ludum it	(Latin)

Two points need be made here. Firstly, the Present Simple is a comparatively rare tense relative to the above uses in other European languages (cf. Leech 1971:64). Secondly, the Present Progressive is often a better translation in English, e.g.:

<u>Peter is going to school tomorrow</u>

Poutsma sees both of these points except that he attributes volition and coercion as well as fixed plan to the Present Simple. He fails to see any idea of "pre-plannedness" behind such examples as:

<u>I am orderly tomorrow</u> (according to the plan drawn up by the sergeant)

<u>I am 55 next week</u> (according to chronological "plan" of nature)

<u>It is ten to one but that you and I are thrown together again in the course of a few years.</u> (Jane Austin) (imagined plan, i.e. predestination)

As indicated above by the present writer's comments in the parentheses, Poutsma like many others fails to make a significant semantic generalisation and takes the idea of "plan" too literally (Poutsma 1928, vol. 2:249ff.). As far as the Present Progressive is concerned, Poutsma fails to present it as basically a less formal version of preplannedness, where plan is to be understood in the abstract sense of plan, decision or mutual arrangement (cf. Sharwood-Smith 1972). For him it is a marker of the immediate future or of the future already in preparation or contemplated as being so. He does not allow:

<u>I am writing to you tomorrow</u>

with "the bulk of verbs", which do not admit of the Progressive form. In fact, this example is a good way of demonstrating the formality difference:

<u>I am writing to you</u> tomorrow (informal)

> I write to you tomorrow (very formal and uncommon in this context)

Note also:

> I'm looking forward to your letter (as between friends)
>
> I look forward to your letter (as in business correspondence--formal)

Jespersen (1961:297) makes the misleading statement that the use of the present tenses indicates the influence of the same point of view. If future reference is apparent in the context, there is no need to use future auxiliaries in this view. Interestingly enough, the same view crops up in generative semantics (see Lakoff 1970, Jenkins 1972, Binnick 1972). This may be true of Danish and other languages but not of English except in subordinate clauses after if, when, after, etc. Elsewhere he notes the preplanned sense of the Present Simple but makes the mistake of saying that it alternates with will as in:

> Tomorrow I leave England. You will never see me again.

As indicated in the next chapter the status (or illocutionary force to borrow a performative term) of these two sentences is quite different. He also says that is here is an example of future reference in:

> It is here that I shall die

which is a moot point to say the least. With regard to the progressive form he makes roughly the same remarks as Poutsma.

Palmer (1965:89ff.) clearly states the distinction between the two present tenses, classifying the progressive form as intention. Plans or decisions made by the speaker may be seen as intentions whereas the simple present tends to denote plans fixed by other people and not in the control of the speaker (e.g. timetables). The durational aspect associated with the progressive "extended" form is discernible, according to Palmer, in either the lasting nature of the intention or of the planned activity itself. By seeing things in terms of intention, Palmer does not quite see that informality is a more significant aspect of the meaning. For example:

<u>The board of directors is meeting tomorrow for a quick consultation</u> is quite possible. The speaker's intention is not involved necessarily, nor is the meeting seen as a lasting event. What decides the use of the progressive form is simply informality. The attitude adopted to the meaning is relaxed or casual or simply neutral: presumably this is a function of some deeper meaning of the progressive. To use the present simple would automatically inject a note of formality into the statement.. What matters then is the conditions of usage rather than the nature of the plan itself which may, in fact, be very serious and solemn in itself. However, Leech (1971:57-9) sees that intention is not involved and also that the plan, in the progressive form, may be regarded as alterable and under the control of the subject.

With the use of a present tense in future reference it is obvious that the context, i.e. the discourse, the situation or the speakers' knowledge of the real world plays a role in indicating that it is in fact future and not present reference. Crystal (1966) found in analysing actual texts that there was a very high occurrence of future adverbials and that in fact in 70% of cases the adverbial was required for a correct interpretation. Wilkins (1972a:32ff.) suggested this would be valuable information for language teaching. It should be noted, however, that the occurrence in written text of these adverbials is probably much higher than it would be if the text were all conversational and all the extra cues of spoken interchange were available. Also, a parallel use of the present tense in the native (European) language would guide the learner in using the English tenses, as far as adverbials are concerned.

Another factor which is not mentioned in grammars is the effect of intonation on giving information relevant to future reference. Chafe wrote an extremely interesting article on language and memory (1973) where he indicated that there might be linguistic evidence for three degrees of memory (instead of the standard two in psychology: short and long term). According to the placement of the time adverbial and the distribution of stress, the speaker may indicate whether the state or event in the past took place very recently (in surface memory), later (in shallow memory) or later still in the past (in deep memory). On a parallel with this he suggested more tentatively that the same process works <u>for expectation</u> (on a parallel with memory), giving surface, shallow and deep expectation. Although no change of verbal form is required to get these distinctions it seems that this would be extremely valuable for the teaching of spoken English at an advanced level. (Such suprasegmental phonological information will not be discussed here although it would belong to a more totally comprehensive treatment of all aspects of future reference.)

2.3. Concluding Remarks

Since the vague, often informative but loosely organised treatments of the early grammarians, the trend has been towards narrowing down the lists of meanings, "modernising" the traditional will/shall paradigm and distinguishing the syntactic and the semantic characteristics of the verbs. Semantic analyses have concentrated on explicating the modal system while those with an interest in the needs of language teaching have cast their net wider and included all the forms treated above under the general category of future time. Despite the simplifications and generalisations achieved to date, the recurring obstacle is still the problem of isolating basic meanings of verbals (if indeed they exist) from their context. It is always informative to know how a verbal form is used in English but some strict if arbitrary distinctions need to be made between basic meaning and meaning supplied by the context (including the lexical meaning of the main verb). After all, a statement like:

I will jump off the chair

may be used to mean a warning, a threat, an intention or a straight prediction according to the circumstances. It is very confusing to have, say, these four meanings listed on equal terms as "meanings of will". Ehrman's use of the notion of basic meaning is therefore very promising, but it needs at the very least to be extended beyond the modals themselves to all forms of future reference. The motivation for this, as has been discussed elsewhere is pedagogical and psychological. It may be argued that there is no such thing as basic meaning and that the meaning of a sentence is a subtle interplay between a whole set of meanings in the sentence, the text and the outside world. For the present purposes, however, it will be assumed that basic meanings exist and that they are to be exploited. The analysis to follow will not give a totally exhaustive account of future reference in English, nor indeed of verbal forms. It will, however, give <u>some</u> account, but within the general aim of presenting a system for pedagogical grammar.

CHAPTER THREE

3.0. A PEDAGOGICAL GRAMMAR OF FUTURE REFERENCE

3.1. Preliminaries

In the preceding chapters a global integrated approach to the problem of writing pedagogical grammar has been set out. The last chapter reviewed the problems of future reference which has been chosen as the topic for illustrating the type of pedagogical grammar discussed. This illustration is just a sample of a more comprehensive treatment of future reference within the grammar as a whole. It concentrates, as the last chapter did, on certain common verbal forms used in future reference. Although the grammar as a whole provides a systematic syntactic description of English, this sample will deal with the more important notional parts, i.e. the semantic and pragmatic sections. The sample will also be monolingual although much of the explanation could be in the target language if it were contrastively orientated. Also there would be intralanguage, notional comparisons in that case. Here, certain technical points should be made. Firstly, in this particular illustration there will be no references to source works, although the debts to McIntosh, Leech, Thorne and Ehrman will be obvious. In a full-scale grammar all the modal auxiliaries would have to appear in the future reference category (as well as elsewhere). Secondly, certain statements will be marked with two asterisks (**). This simply indicates a reference to another part of the grammar which is of course purely hypothetical at the present time.

As regards the semantic section, as much general situation-free information will be concentrated here, leaving the pragmatic section as much as possible reserved for points of specific usage. In the pragmatic section only those specific situations which need to be described in detail will occupy more than a brief comment. In many cases a few words will be necessary to describe the given pragmatic conditions since they will relate directly, in an obvious manner, to the learner's experience of the real world. Some information about "usage" will appear in both the semantic and pragmatic sections since it is not always easy to say whether such information if "general" or relatively situation-free.

The formalisations in the grammar will observe the psychological strictures outlined in the first chapter. The categories and subcategories of future reference will be treated as organisers both in the context of the grammar and as potential devices for teaching. The most abstract and generalised categories will serve as advance expository organisers under which the subsequent information may be subsumed. It must be taken for granted that a certain amount of preliminary information is available in the grammar, showing how this can be exploited in the classroom and textbook.

Finally, it should be noted that a two sentence analysis is used in the semantic section following a recent development of Thorne (as explained in two lectures given in Poznań, 1974). It was used to explicate certain notions such as various past tense decisions in English, the distinction between <u>that</u>- and <u>to</u>-clauses, and certain quantifiers problems. For example, the tense choices as between the Present Perfect, the Preterite and the Past Perfect were neatly shown as follows:

<u>He has left</u> = it Pres be the case: he Past leave
<u>He left</u>   = it Past be the case: he Pres leave
<u>He had left</u> = it Past be the case: he Past leave

This technique will be expanded and adapted to explicate notions of future reference.

3.2. A Monolingual Notional Analysis of English Verbal Forms of Future Reference: a Sample

3.2.1. The Semantic Section

0—0 F U T U R E R E F E R E N C E
Ways of Looking at the Future and How These Ways Are
Expressed in English

When we talk about the future in English, there are two basic views that the language makes available to us:

        A. The FUTURE-FUTURE VIEW

        B. The PRESENT-FUTURE VIEW

A. <u>The Future-Future View</u>

The future state or event, as we see it in our mind's eye, is viewed

as belonging completely to the future. In other words, we momentarily
concentrate on some situation. For example, if we take Archibald's
being at the party tomorrow as an example, we may formalise this view
as follows:

    It <u>FUTURE</u> be the case: FUTURE (Archibald be at the party)

The future state or event is marked off in parentheses.

B. <u>The Present-Future View</u>

The future state or event is viewed as being relevant to the <u>Present</u> in
some way. Notice that we say <u>viewed</u>. We are not talking about logical or
common sense judgements. We are talking about the <u>momentary psychological
attitude</u> in the speaker (or writer). Here the state or event may already
be in the process of taking place, or it may have been planned or decided
upon. This fact is taken into consideration in this view of the future.
The formalisation is as follows:

    It <u>PRESENT</u> be the case: FUTURE (Archibald be at the party)

A. and B. <u>The Two Views</u>

To sum up, we have two fundamental views of the future: the first (A)
where we concentrate on the state or event occurring in the future. We
have, as it were, <u>both eyes closed</u> (momentarily), to the present; the
second (B), where we see the future state or event as a development or
consequence of something we already know about in the present. Here we
have, as it were, <u>one eye open</u> on the present. These two views may be
represented symbolically as the both-eyes-closed (●—●) and the one-eye-
open (O—●) view:

```
                        . A. ●—● (the FUTURE-FUTURE)
                      ..
FUTURE REFERENCE -----.
                      ..
                       . B. ○—● (the PRESENT-FUTURE)
```

These two fundamental perspectives will now be examined in more detail.

●—● (the Future-Future)

English has various ways of talking about the past, the present and about time-neutral situations ** (references to appropriate sections). For example:

1. <u>John is swimming the Channel</u> (now)
2. <u>John swims (every day)</u> / <u>John swims well (generally)</u>
3. <u>John has been swimming all day</u>
4. <u>John has swum the Channel</u> (already)
5. <u>John swam the Channel</u> (yesterday)
6. <u>John had swum</u> (the day before)
7. <u>John had been swimming</u> (the day before)

All the ideas expressed in 1-7 are theoretically possible as ideas viewed in the future. The exponents are: <u>will</u> (in all persons), <u>shall</u> (in the first person) and the contraction <u>'ll</u>. Due to the complexity of the verb phrases the past time references (3-7) are normally expressed by the simplest form, i.e. <u>will have</u> plus the progressive aspect if necessary. In other words, <u>will have had been</u> may be discounted. The above examples viewed as the Future-Future could therefore be realised as follows:

-1. <u>John will be swimming the Channel</u> (on that morning)
-2. <u>John will swim every day</u>/<u>will swim well</u> (some day)

-3. <u>John will have been swimming all day</u>

-4. <u>John will have swum the Channel</u> (already)

-5. <u>John will have swum the Channel</u> (the day before)

-6. <u>John will have swum the Channel</u> (the day before that)

-7. <u>John will have been swimming</u> (the day before that)

The Future-Future may be subdivided into:

    Aa. The GENERAL Future-Future

    Ab. The PROJECTED Future-Future

Aa. The state or event viewed in the future is genuinely not presently occurring, something that may only occur in the future, e.g. the above seven examples.

Ab. The relevant state or event is <u>actually</u> present or past or time-neutral. The speaker (or writer) chooses, however, to view it as relevant to the future. An imaginary future state or event is hypothesised momentarily by "projecting" a present or time-neutral state or event into the future. Take the following examples:

  8. <u>Oil floats on water</u> (time-neutral)

  9. <u>This hall seats 500</u> (time-neutral)

10. <u>That's Waldek at the door</u> (present)

11. <u>Jacek is now in Lublin</u> (present)

12. <u>Jim is now sleeping in Bloomington</u> (present)

13. <u>That's enough to last me till Christmas</u> (present)

14. <u>Ewa has arrived in Utrecht</u> (past-cum-present)

All these statements may be given a hypothetical future dimension by using the auxiliary will. The speaker momentarily distances himself from the present moment by means of hypothetical future reference (see note on "will-contingency" below). Thus:

-8. Oil will float on water (If you want to test this, you'll find it's true)

-9. This hall will seat 500 (Count the chairs and you will see)

-10. That will be Waldek at the door (In a moment we will see him)

-11. Jacek will now be in Lublin (If we wanted to check this, we would find him there)

-12. Jim will now be sleeping in Bloomington (ditto)

-13. That will be enough to last me till Christmas (In a few months time, I'll still have some left)

-14. Ewa will have arrived in Utrecht (by now) (If I phone her, she will answer)

We should note: a. past reference in the Projected Future-Future may additionally employ the time adverbial phrase by now (cf. -13.). This links it with the General Future-Future which may employ a parallel construction, e.g. by tomorrow, by next year, etc., and b. shall is not used in this sense (e.g. *That shall be Waldek), although the contraction 'll is.

NOTES:

Will-contingency

A general semantic characteristic of will should be noted here. This has to do with a semantic implication that will may have in all its occurrences. This may be called contingency: the state or event referred to is felt to be dependent on or related in some way to another state or event (often in the future). This has in fact been well illustrated above by the effect that the presence of <u>will</u> has on sentences which logically refer to the present (e.g. 10 and -10) in the kind of extended paraphrases they imply (see the explications in parentheses in -8 to -14). It also explains why it is <u>will</u> that is the standard form used in the main clauses of conditional sentences. Examples:

15. <u>I will be sick if you go on feeding me that rubbish.</u>
16. <u>I will give you the book as long as you promise to take care of it.</u>

Emotional potential

Another general semantic observation is that emphatic stress placed on <u>will</u> and <u>shall</u> expresses an emotional attitude on the part of the speaker, the nature of which is determined pragmatically (see Pragmatic Section).

O—● (the Present-Future)

Here, the speaker (or writer) directly relates the future state or event to <u>something he already knows about in the present</u>. This present knowledge may be expressed in a general way or in a more specific way, giving us the two subdivisions of the Present-Future view:

> Ba. The GENERAL Present-Future
> Bb. The PROGRAMMED Present-Future

Ba. The general Present-Future is expressed by the form <u>going to</u>. Examples:

17. <u>It's going to rain</u>

18. <u>John's going to come later</u>
19. <u>I am going to be sick</u>
20. <u>I am going to hit you</u>
21. <u>There is going to be a population crisis in 1990</u>

The above statements may be regarded as confident assertions of one kind or another, the future states or events not contingent on any other state or event. The present knowledge here may be of the following sort:

-17. Black clouds are now in the sky
-18. John's intention now
-19. Present symptoms
-20. My intention and determination now
-21. Present indications of the birth rate

The notion of general Present-Future and that of Future-Future may be illustrated by the following pair of statements. Note the effect of will-contingency:

<u>I am going to be sick and there is nothing anyone can do to prevent it</u>
<u>I will be sick if you force me to eat all that revolting cake</u>

Bb. The Programmed Present-Future is expressed by the forms <u>be to</u> and by the two Present Tenses in English (Simple and Progressive). The knowledge of the relevant present factors is more specifically knowledge of an existing <u>programme</u>. This programme is to be understood in a wide sense as covering fixed decisions, arrangements as well as large scale plans and programmes. Although this very often refers to man-made "programmes", it may occasionally refer to regular law-governed phenomena in nature.

Examples:

> The President is arriving at midday
>
> The President is to arrive at midday
>
> The President arrives at midday

It is, however, necessary to distinguish two broad subdivisions of the Programmed Present-Future: Bb (INFORMAL) and Bb (FORMAL). As may be seen above, the President's arrival, which is a large scale fixed programmed event outside the speaker's control, may be viewed both ways. The exponent of the informal way (Bb (INFORMAL)) is the Present Progressive. The exponents of the formal way (Bb (FORMAL)) are the Present Simple and be to. As may be expected, small scale plans, arrangements and decisions tend to be expressed informally, large scale plans, regarded as inalterable, formally. Examples:

22. I'm coming by train, by the way (INFORMAL)
23. Geoff is taking Colin's place (INFORMAL)
24. The ceremony is to take place in Brussels (FORMAL)
25. The plane leaves Poznań at 11:40 (FORMAL)

It should be noted that:

a. the formal/informal distinction is associated with the absence or presence of the Progressive -ing form, respectively (cf. I write/am writing to inform you).

b. with the present tenses a future time adverbial or some other cue in the discourse or situation will disambiguate the time reference.

●━● + ○━● (A COMBINED VIEW) (A + B)

The English language, in one particular case, can make available to the speaker (or writer) a view which combines the Future-Future view with the Programmed Present-Future. This amounts to informing the listener (or reader) that at some time in the future you will be in a position to inform him of a future plan. Look at the following example:

26. I will be driving to Kazimierz tomorrow

This might be interpreted simply as a Future-Future view; but there is another separate, combined interpretation which may be paraphrased roughly as:

-26. There will be a time in the future (tomorrow) where I will be able to say to you: "I am driving to Kazimierz today"

In this case the Kazimierz journey has not yet begun at the chosen point in the future. I am driving to Kazimierz here is in itself an informal Programmed-Future, not a statement of what is happening already. In one sense it is Future- Future, but in another sense informing someone of a future plan is tantamount to informing him of a present plan. In this latter sense, it is informal Programmed-Future. This combined view has been termed the "Future-as-a-matter-of-course". It enables the speaker to disassociate the subject of the sentence from any of the potential connotations of personal responsibility that may arise in certain situations. This may be best illustrated by the following questions:

27. Will you be driving to Kazimierz tomorrow?

The questioner is specifically interested in the future event because (for example) he wishes to ask the driver for a lift. At the same time, he does not want either the listener to drive to

Kazimierz especially to give him a lift or to arrange his journey to fit in with his (the speaker's) plans. In other words he does not want to force him to say:

<u>I will drive you there if you want a lift</u>

or

<u>Yes, I'm going to drive there</u>. (<u>I see you now want a lift tomorrow</u>)
The speaker wants to know, not about any present plan now, but about programmed activity <u>with specific reference to the future</u> (and not dependent on the present situation in any way) (see also Pragmatic Section below). Present relevance is thereby "suppressed".

The exponents of the combined form are <u>will</u>, <u>'ll</u> (and <u>shall</u> in the first person) plus the Progressive form <u>be+-ing</u>.

<u>AN OVERVIEW</u>

The notions available to the user of English in Future Reference are as follows:

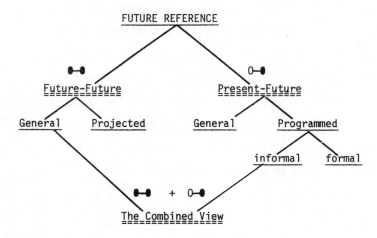

The exponents of these notions are listed in the appropriate parts of the Semantic Section. **For a full account of their syntactic behaviour, see the Syntactic Section.

3.2.2. The Pragmatic Section

When the speaker (or writer) refers to the future, he may be said in most cases to be making a PREDICTION. In other words, he predicts a state or event for the listener (or reader). But he may wish to use this general meaning of prediction for particular purposes:

1. Information about WISHES AND INTENTIONS

When we say:

   It is going to rain!

our knowledge of the world tells us that it does not intend or wish to rain. However, wherever our knowledge of the world tells us that the subject is capable of wishes and intentions and our knowledge of the situation tells us that a wish or intention is likely, then we accordingly may interpret an expression of future reference also as a wish or intention. Examples:

   Hamish is going to finish the whisky bottle

The "programme" here may, of course, be not Hamish's own. His drinking companions may have decided this for him. But if we do not have any information about that, we may well interpret this as:

   Hamish intends to finish the whisky bottle

However, if we consider the following:

   Hamish is going to fall over

our knowledge of the real world, through our understanding of the verb fall over, will normally rule out the interpretation:

> Hamish intends to fall over

In this unlikely event (--Hamish may be acting--) we might well use the verb intend to make our interpretation clear. The same general rule applies for all exponents of future reference, e.g.:

> Hamish'll fall over
>
> Hamish'll finish the whisky bottle

Intentions and wishes are especially likely in the situation where we are a. talking about ourselves and b. talking about the normal objects of wishes and intentions. Examples:

> I am going to finish the bottle
>
> I'll finish the bottle
>
> Right, I start work tomorrow!

However, the volition of the subject is always implied when will (uncontracted is inserted into an if-clause in a conditional sentence:

> If they will tell us, we will certainly pass the news on.

2. Special Types of Wishes and Intentions

a. Promises

The speaker (or writer) personally guarantees the predicted state or event. The listener (or reader) understands that he is in a position to make that guarantee and accepts it as a statement of self-obligation. Promises are typically expressed by exponents of the Future-Future:

> I'll do it by tomorrow
>
> My son will be at school on time

Note that in a promise situation the <u>speaker</u> (or <u>writer</u>), not the subject, makes the promise.

b. <u>Expression of Determination, Commands (Promises)</u>

Here, in speech, emphatic stress is often placed on the verb, thus:

<u>I 'will be there on time</u>

<u>They are 'going to listen to me whether they like it or not</u>

<u>I 'shall be there</u>

The stress cannot fall on <u>be</u> (this asserts the truth value).

Thus:

<u>You are to 'sit down and be 'quiet!</u>

<u>He's 'coming, I tell you!</u>

c. <u>Expression of Humour, Surprise at the Subject's Characteristic Activity or Acceptance of Something Disagreeable</u>

This is a use of the Projected Future-Future:

<u>She will sit there for hours doing nothing. Whenever you talk to her she won't say anything. If you go and see her, you'll see what I mean.</u>

<u>Boys will be boys!</u>

<u>Accidents will happen!</u>

3. <u>More on the Combined View</u> (see Semantic Section)

This notion may be used generally where there is a matching of two plans in the future:

<u>I shall be painting the kitchen at six o'clock, so call round at six sharp and we will start it together</u>

Note that this is NOT the Future-Future interpretation where at six the speaker has already started painting. At six sharp the painting is still Programmed Future. The Combined form may indeed be used simply as post-future. A point in the future is selected and the state or event is viewed as taking place after that point, e.g.:

<u>When will you be painting your kitchen?</u>

But its potential as help in coordinating two plans is evident.

4. <u>Be-to Obligation</u> ** (see also Expression of Obligation)

The form <u>be to</u> (Programmed Present-Future (Formal)) carries with it a potential implication that the subject is obliged to undertake some future activity. In other words, the plan implies an obligation placed on the subject by someone else in authority over the subject. Thus:

<u>He is to carry out the orders on Friday</u>

<u>They are to come on Monday</u>

If we take, for example, the Present Simple versions:

<u>He carries out the orders on Friday</u>

<u>They come on Monday</u>

the plan may be regarded as fixed and inalterable, but no statement is made about any idea of obligation (whether it exists or not).

3.3. Concluding Remarks

3.3.1. Linguistic

If we consider the proliferation of meanings that may occur in describing the semantics of even <u>will</u> and <u>shall</u> alone, any simplifying framework should be welcome, provided it agrees with native speaker intuitions. If this can be extended to cover a larger area, e.g. future reference, so much the better. The decision to separate notions from outward forms is not new. However, it has been carried to a logical conclusion. The forms have already been well described. It is now time that notions should also be dealt with in a systematic way. Time reference has been dealt with independently of tense. However, no system would survive if it did not observe the fact that there is correspondence between time and tense. A notional framework that took no account of the forms used in the language would be either seriously in error or simply uneconomical. In the present system, therefore, there may be observed a fairly close relationship between form and meaning. For example, <u>will</u> forms are associated with the Future-Future view. What is most important is that this notion-form correspondence should be more covert than overt. A notional analysis describes notions first and foremost and then afterwards deals with the various exponents of those notions. In this we can provide the learner with what he needs; the conceptual apparatus reflected in the language and not just a list of forms with ad-hoc semantic descriptions. The semantic-pragmatic description, interpreted liberally, provides the teacher and learner with an important insight, namely that a useful distinction consists in separating basic meanings and then in seeing how these meanings may be used in particular situations. <u>Will</u> has proved to be the classic example.

3.3.2. Psychological

The overview diagram on page 98 in 3.2.1. provides the teacher and textbook writer (as well as the casual reader) with a network of organisers. These will allow the learner to build up the conceptual system of future reference with its exponents stage by stage. The highest advance organisers provide a beachhead for the rest of the information to be based on. The grammar thus provides a ready-made programme in condensed form. This is for the teacher and textbook writer to exploit as he wishes, developing the semantic and pragmatic themes according to his special needs. The grammar, however, should lend itself particularly to exploitation by those of the cognitive persuasion in learning psychology. Keuleers (1974) applies and develops Engels' ideas of <u>mediators</u>, which are language teaching organisers of various sorts and help the learner to bridge the gap between the conscious application of rules and the automatic fluency that characterises the native speaker. They provide the learner with a metalanguage (Keuleers 1974:253) for creating novel utterances in the target language. They should be <u>complete</u>, <u>concise</u>, <u>accurate</u> and <u>appealing</u> (Keuleers 1974:253). The mediators actually used in the sample are semantic meadators. In Keuleers terms, some of them are <u>pictorial</u>, cf. the two-eye symbols, but most of them are <u>explicit</u>, e.g. <u>Future-Future</u>, <u>Programmed Future</u>, etc. These could easily be adapted to <u>cognitive drills</u> which require highly condensed semantic information for instantaneous application by the learner (who has to create sentences by means of them). The sample provides both material for <u>inclusive</u> mediators which are lexical items inserted into the drill model as cues (e.g. <u>by now</u>, <u>by tomorrow</u>) and also for <u>annexed</u> mediators where condensed semantic information is set a little up from the line (e.g. ...$^{\text{Pres-Fut}}$, ...$^{\text{Program-Formal}}$, etc.). However, more traditional cognitive exercises could equally well be developed from the sample using the explanatory extended paraphrases (e.g. <u>I will be sick...if I eat any more</u>) to teach the sorts of contexts needed for the use of the exponents of Future Reference. The organisers themselves provide cue material, and paraphrases of these notions could easily be developed. For example, the notion "programme" would suggest cues like: <u>What do you plan to do today?</u>, <u>What has John decided?</u>, <u>What have they arranged for Monday?</u>, etc., requiring the learner to respond with the appropriate (programmed) future exponent.

3.3.3. Sociological

The sample does not provide the large amount of sociolinguistic information needed to fully explicate all the shades of usage. It does, however, provide something to start with and something that is organised. The emphasis on structure without regard for its use has been offset and information about English has been arranged in a way that will facilitate the development of communicative competence. The pragmatic section in particular provides a basis for relating the elements and patterns of English to actual speech acts that the learner wants to understand and perform. A source book of English usage is still vital for the construction of proper teaching materials however. The more such books are related to the dynamic version of pedagogical grammar here described, the better.

3.3.4. Final Statement

In the first part of this dissertation, the concept of pedagogical grammar was discussed and one particular interpretation arrived at after reviewing the present linguistic, psychological and sociological stock of theories judged to have potential relevance for language pedagogy. While recognizing the practicability of the safer and more usual interpretation, i.e. the idea of a simplified eclectic version of more theoretical descriptions, it was decided that a more unified principled description was worth attempting. Such a pedagogical grammar might contribute to language teaching in a constructive way and also help to establish language pedagogy as an independent field of inquiry. Whereas the dominating theories of the fifties produced systematic accounts of language structure and a demonstration of the importance of habit-formation in language learning, it was noted that certain vital aspects-- vital for language pedagogy, that is--of language had been left relatively unexplored. Meaning, as conveyed by language, was characterised in this dissertation as having priority over structure and support was looked for in cognitive psychology for this assumption. Given the fact that the learner needs to know both the structure <u>and</u> the meaning behind the structure of the target language, meaning nevertheless comes first as having the largest number of links with information already present in the learner's cognitive structure. Moreover, the learner's conscious acquaintance with structure is primarily a means to the end of finding out how to convey meaning. The paradox is that due to the inherent regularity of syntax and the complexity of semantics, the analysis and presentation of language structure is much more developed at the moment than that of language meaning. The aim of this dissertation has been to make a small and very modest step towards correcting this situation. The study of one particularly difficult problem area, i.e. time reference has been used to this end. Although such a notional analysis could quite well be incorporated into a grammar where systematic accounts of both syntax and semantics are presented as two equal aspects of the target language it is nevertheless argued that language structure should be seen first and foremost through language meaning rather than vice versa facilitating transfer from the native to the target language. This kind of approach may even be valid for theoretical analyses; it is more confidently asserted for pedagogical descriptions.

BIBLIOGRAPHY

AGARD, F. and R.J. PIETRO. (1965) The Grammatical Structure of English and Italian. Chicago: The University of Chicago Press.

ALLEN, H.B. (1958) Readings in Applied English Linguistics. New York: Appleton-Century-Crofts.

ALLEN, P.B.J. and P. van Buren (eds.). (1971) Chomsky: Selected Readings. Oxford: Oxford University Press.

ALLEN, R.L. (1966) The Verb System of Present Day American English. The Hague: Mouton.

AUSTIN, J.L. (1962) How to Do Things with Words. Oxford: Oxford University Press.

AUSUBEL, D.P. (1968) Educational Psychology: A Cognitive View. New York: Holt, Rinehart and Winston.

BACH, E. and R.T. HARMS (eds.). (1968) Universals in Linguistic Theory. New York: Holt, Rinehart and Winston.

BAZELL, C.E., J.C. CATFORD, M.A.K. HALLIDAY and R.H. ROBINS (eds.). (1966) In Memory of J.R. Firth. London: Longmans.

BERLIN, I. (ed.).(1973) Essays on J.L. Austin. Oxford: Oxford University Press.

BINNICK, R.I. (1972) "Will and Be Going To II" in Peranteau et al. 1972: 3-10.

BLOOMFIELD, L. (1933) Language. New York: Holt, Rinehart and Winston.

---. (1942) Outline Guide for the Practical Study of Languages. New York: Linguistic Society of America.

BOYD, J. and J.P. THORNE. (1969) "The Semantics of Modal Verbs" in *Journal of Linguistics* 5. 57-74.

BULL, W.E. (1960) *Time, Tense and the Verbs*. Berkeley: University of California.

CATTELL, N.R. (1969) *The New English Grammar*. Cambridge, Mass.: MIT Press.

CHAFE, W.L. (1973) "Language and Memory" in *Language* 49. 261-282.

CHASTAIN, K. (1971) *The Development of Foreign Language Skills*. Philadelphia: The Centre for Curriculum Development.

CHERRY, C. (1971) (Reprint). *On Human Communication*. Cambridge, Mass.: MIT Press.

CHOMSKY, N. (1957) *Syntactic Structures*. The Hague: Mouton.

---. (1959) "Review" of Skinner's *Verbal Behaviour*. *Language* 35. 26-58.

---. (1965) *Aspects of the Theory of Syntax*. The Hague: Mouton.

---. (1966) "Linguistic Theory", a paper read at the Northeast Conference on the Teaching of Foreign Languages. 1965. in Allen and Van Buren 1971: 152-159.

CLOSE, R.A. (1962) English as a Foreign Language. London: Allen and Unwin.

---. (1969) "Problems of the Future Tense (1)" in *English Language Teaching* XXIV: 225-232.

---. (1970a) "Problems of the Future Tense (2)" in *English Language Teaching* XXV: 43-49.

---. (1970b) *The Future*. London: Longmans.

CORDER, S.P. (1967) "The Significance of Learner's Errors" in *International Review of Applied Linguistics* 4: 161-170.

CORDER, S.P. (1973) *Introducing Applied Linguistics*. Harmondsworth: Penguin.

CRAIG, R.C. (1966) *The Psychology of Learning in the Classroom*. London: Collier Macmillan.

CRYSTAL, D. (1966) "Specification and English Tenses" in *Journal of Linguistics* 2: 1-34.

---. (1971) *Linguistics*. Harmondsworth: Penguin.

CURRIE, W.B. (1973) *New Directions in Teaching English Language*. London: Longmans.

DAVIDSON, D. and G. HARMAN (eds.) (1972) *Semantics of Natural Language*. Dordrecht: Reidel.

DIVER, W. (1963) "The Chronological System of the English Verb" in *Word* 20: 141-181.

---. (1964) "The Modal System of the English Verb" in *Word* 20: 332-352.

EHRMAN, M. (1966). *The Meaning of Modals in Present Day American English*. The Hague: Mouton.

ENGELS, L.K. (1970) "The Function of Grammar in the Teaching of English as a Foreign Language" in *ITL* 10: 11-24.

FILLMORE, C.J. and D.T. LANGENDOEN. (1971) *Studies in Linguistic Semantics*. New York: Holt, Rinehart and Winston.

FIRTH, J.R. (1951) "Modes of Meaning" in Firth. 1958: 190-216.

---. (1958) (Reprint) *Papers in Linguistics 1934-1951*. Oxford: Oxford University Press.

FISHMAN, J.A. (1969). *Sociolinguistics*. Rowley: Newbury House.

FERGUSON, L.W. (1973) "Locutionary and Illocutionary Acts" in Berlin 1973: 160-187.

FRIED, V. (ed.). (1972) *The Prague School of Linguistics and Language Teaching*. Oxford: Oxford University Press.

FRIES, C.C. (1940) *American English Grammar*. New York: Appleton.

---. (1954) "Meaning and Linguistic Analysis" in Allen. 1958: 98-111.

---. (1957) *The Structure of English*. London: Longmans.

GARNER, R. (1971) "Presupposition in Philosophy and Linguistics" in Fillmore and Langendoen 1971: 23-45.

GEORGE, H.V. (1972) *Common Errors in Language Learning*. Rowley: Newbury House.

GLEITMAN, L.R. and H. GLEITMAN. (1970) *Phrase and Paraphrase*. New York: Mouton.

GREENE, J. (1972) *Psycholinguistics* Harmondsworth: Penguin.

GUMPERZ, J.J. and D. HYMES (eds.). (1970) *Directions in Sociolinguistics*. New York: Holt, Rinehart and Winston.

HALL, B. (1964) "Adverbial Subordinate Clauses", a working paper *W-07241*. Bedford: Mitre Corporation.

HALLIDAY, M.A.K. (1961) "Categories of the Theory of Grammar" in *Word* 17: 241-291.

---. (1970) "Language Structure and Language Function" in Lyons. 1970: 140-166.

HALLIDAY, M.A.K., A. McINTOSH and P. STREVENS. (1964) *The Linguistic Sciences and Language Teaching*. London: Longmans.

HYMES, D. (1972) "On Communicative Competence" in Pride and Holmes. 1972: 269-294.

JACOBS, R.A. and P.S. ROSENBAUM (eds.). (1970) *Readings in Transformational Grammar* Waltham: Ginn.

JAKOBOVITS, L. (1970) Foreign Language Learning. Rowley: Newbury House.

JENKINS, L. (1972) "Will-Deletion" in Peranteau et al. 1972: 173-183.

JESPERSEN, O. (1933) Essentials of English Grammar. London: Allen and Unwin.

---. (1961) (Reprint) A Modern English Grammar. London: Allen and Unwin.

---. (1965) (Revised) The Philosophy of Grammar. New York: Norton.

JOOS, M. (1964) The English Verb: Form and Meaning. Madison and Milwaukee: University of Wisconsin Press.

KAKIETEK, P. (1969) Modal Verbs in Shakespeare's English. Unpublished Ph.D. dissertation. Poznań. Adam Mickiewicz University.

---. (1970a) "Observations on the Modals 'will' and 'shall'" in Studia Anglica Posnaniensia 2: 51-59.

---. (1970b) "Review" of Ehrman 1966 in Studia Anglica Posnaniensia 2: 113-116.

---. (1970c) "May and Might in Shakespeare's English" in Linguistics 64: 26-35.

KELLY, L.G. (1969) Twenty-Five Centuries of Language Teaching. Rowley: Newbury House.

KEULEERS, A. (1971) "Cognitive Drills for the Language Laboratory" in ITL 14: 29-41.

---. (1974) Insight, Automatisation and Creativity in Foreign Language Learning. (Ph.D. dissertation) Louvain: Katholieke Universiteit.

KRUISINGA, E. (1925) A Handbook of Present Day English: Part II (4th Ed.) Over den Dom te Utrecht: Kemink en Zoon.

KRZESZOWSKI, T.P.K. (1970) Teaching English to Polish Learners. Warszawa: Państwowe Wydawnictwo Naukowe.

KRZESZOWSKI, T.P.K. (1971) "Equivalence, Congruence and Deep Structure" in Nickel. 1971: 37-49.

LADO, R. (1964) Language Teaching. New York: McGraw-Hill.

LAKOFF, G. "On Generative Semantics" in Steinberg and Jacobsen 1971: 232-296.

LAKOFF, R. (1970) "Tense and its Relation to Participants" in Language 46: 838-849.

---. (1972a) "Language in Context" in Language 48: 907-927.

---. (1972b) "The Pragmatics of Modality" in Peranteau et al. 1972: 229-247.

---. (1973) "Linguistic Theory and the Real World", a paper given at the TESOL conference, Denver, Colorado. March 1973.

LANGENDOEN, D.T. and H.B. SAVIN. (1971) "The Projection Problem for Presuppositions" in Fillmore and Langendoen 1971: 55-63.

LAWLER, J. and L. SELINKER. (1971) "On Paradoxes, Rules, and Research in Second Language Learning" in Language Learning 21: 27-45.

LEECH, G.N. (1966) English in Advertising. London: Longmans.

---. (1971) Meaning and the English Verb. London: Longmans.

LYONS, J. (1963) Structural Semantics. Oxford: Blackwell.

---. (1968) Introduction to Theoretical Linguistics. Cambridge: Cambridge University Press.

---. (1970) New Horizons in Linguistics. Harmondsworth: Penguin.

MARTON, W. (1972a) Nowe horyzonty w nauczaniu jezyków obcych. Warszawa: PZWS.

---. (1972b) "Pedagogical Implications of Contrastive Linguistics". A paper given at the Third International Conference in Copenhagen. August 1972.

McCAWLEY, J.B. (1968) "The Role of Semantics in Grammar" in Bach and Harms 1968: 125-171.

---. (1971) "Tense and Time Reference in English" in Fillmore and Langendoen 1971: 97-118.

McINTOSH, A. (1966) "Predictive Statements" in Bazell et al. 1966: 303-320.

MATHESIUS, V. (1967) "On Problems of the Systematic Analysis of Grammar" in Vachek 1967: 306-320.

MENSIKOVA, A. (1972) "Sentence Patterns in the Theory and Practice of Teaching the Grammar of French as a Foreign Language" in Fried 1972: 29-43.

MILLER, G.E., E. GALANTER and K.H. PRIBRAM. (1970) Plans and the Structure of Behavior. London: Holt, Rinehart and Winston. (first edition 1960).

MITTINS, W.H., M. SALU, M. EDMINSON and S. COYNE. (1970) Attitudes to English Usage. Oxford: Oxford University Press.

MONTAGUE, R. (1972) "Pragmatics and Intensional Logic" in Davidson and Harmon 1972: 142-168.

MORRIS, C. (1964) Signification and Significance. Cambridge, Mass.: MIT Press.

MOUTON (eds.). (1967) To Honor Roman Jakobson. III. The Hague: Mouton.

NICKEL, G. (ed.). (1971a) Papers in Contrastive Linguistics. Cambridge: Cambridge University Press.

---. (1971b) "Contrastive Linguistics and Foreign Language Teaching" in Nickel 1971a: 1-17.

OLLER, J.W., Jr. (1971) "Transformational Grammar, Pragmatics and Language Teaching" in English Teaching Forum 9: 8-12.

OSKARSSON, M. (1972) "The Acquisition of Foreign Language Grammar by Adults". A paper given at the Third International Congress of Applied Linguistics in Copenhagen. August 1972.

---. (1974) "Monolingual and Bilingual Vocabulary Learning: Theoretical Background and Experimental Findings". A paper read at the TIT/IATEFL international conference in Budapest, April 1974.

OTA, A. (1963) Tense and Aspect of Present Day American English. Tokyo: Kenkyusha.

---. (1965) "Review" of Joos 1964 in Language 41: 657-674.

PALMER, F.R. (1965) A Linguistic Study of the English Verb. London: Longmans.

PERANTEAU, P.M., J.N. LEVI and G.C. PHARES (eds.). (1972) Papers from the Eighth Regional Meeting of the Chicago Linguistic Society. Chicago: Chicago Linguistic Society.

PIMSLEUR, P. and T. QUINN. (1971) The Psychology of Second Language Learning. Cambridge: Cambridge University Press.

POUTSMA, H. (1928) A Grammar of Late Modern English. Groningen: Noordhoff.

PRIDE, J.B. and J. HOLMES (eds.). (1972) Sociolinguistics. Harmondsworth: Penguin.

QUIRK, R., S. GREENBAUM, G. LEECH and J. SVARTVIK. (1973) A Grammar of Contemporary English. London: Longmans. (2nd Edition).

RIVERS, W. (1964) The Psychologist and the Foreign Language Teacher. Chicago: University of Chicago Press.

---. (1969) Teaching Foreign Language Skills. Chicago: University of Chicago Press.

ROBERTS, P. (1956) *Patterns of English*. New York: Harcourt, Brace and World.

---. (1962) *English Sentences*. New York: Harcourt, Brace and World.

---. (1967) *A Modern Grammar*. New York: Harcourt, Brace and World.

ROSS, J.R. (1967) "On the Cyclic Nature of English Pronominalization" in Mouton 1967: 1669-1682.

---. (1970) "On Declarative Sentences" in Jacobs and Rosenbaum 1970: 222-273.

SCHLEGOFF, E.A. (1968) "Sequencing in Conversational Openings" in Gumperz and Hymes 1972: 346-381.

SEARLE, J.B. (1970) *Speech Acts*. Cambridge: Cambridge University Press.

---. (1973) "Austin on Locutionary and Illocutionary Acts" in Berlin 1973: 141-160.

SELINKER, L. (1971) "The Psychologically Relevant Data of Second Language Learning" in Pimsleur and Quinn 1971: 35-43.

SHARWOOD SMITH, M.A. (1972) "English Verbs of Future Reference in a Pedagogical Grammar" in *Studia Anglica Posnaniensia* 4: 51-60.

---. (1975) "Aspects of Future Reference in English and Polish" in *Papers* and Studies in Contrastive Linguistics 3 (1974): 90-99. Adam Mickiewicz University, Poznań/Center for Applied Linguistics, Washington. D.C.

SLOBIN, D.I. (1971) *Psycholinguistics*. Illinois: Scott, Foresman.

SMABY, R.M. (1971) *Paraphrase Grammars*. Dordrecht: Reidel.

STALNAKER, R.C. (1972) "Pragmatics" in Davidson and Harmon 1972: 386-397.

STEINBERG, D.D. and L. JAKOBOVITS (eds.). (1971) *Semantics*. Cambridge: Cambridge University Press.

STOCKWELL, R.P., J.D. BOWEN and J.W. MARTIN. (1965) The Grammatical Structures of English and Spanish. Chicago: University of Chicago Press.

STRAWSON, P.F. (1973) "Austin and Logical Meaning" in Berlin 1973: 46-49.

SZWEDEK, A. (1969) The Verb System in Beaumont and Fletcher's Works. Unpublished Ph.D. dissertation. Łódź University.

THOMAS, O. (1965) Transformational Grammar and the Teacher of English. New York: Holt, Rinehart and Winston.

THOMSON, R. (1969) The Psychology of Thinking. Harmondsworth: Penguin.

TREGIDGO, P.S. (1974) "English Tense Usage: a Bull's Eye View" in English Language Teaching 2: 97-107.

TRIM, J.L.M. (1971) "The Analysis of Language Contents". Paper at the Council of Europe Symposium at Rüshlikon 1971.

TWADELL, F. (1965) The English Verb Auxiliary. Second edition, revised. Providence: Brown University Press.

VACHEK, J. (1972) "The Linguistic Theory of the Prague School" in Fried 1972: 11-26.

VAN BUREN, P. (1970) "Traditional Versus Modern Linguistics". Unpublished material used at the Department of Linguistics, Edinburgh University.

VYGOTSKY, L.S. (1962) Thought and Language. Trans. by E. Hanfmann and G. Vakar. Cambridge, Mass.: MIT Press.

WARNOCK, G.J. (1973) "Some types of Performative Utterance" in Berlin 1973: 69-89.

WIDDOWSON, H. (1969) "The Textbook Presentation of Grammar". Unpublished material for use at the Department of Linguistics, Edinburgh University.

WILKINS, D.A. (1971) "Linguistics and the Scientific Study of Language Teaching". A paper presented at the joint ALVA/BAAL seminar.

---. (1972a) <u>Linguistics in Language Teaching</u>. London: Arnold.

---. (1972b) "Grammatical, Situational and Notional Syllabuses". A paper presented at the Third International Congress of Applied Linguistics, Copenhagen. August 1972.

ZANDVOORT, R.W. (1970a) "Three Grammarians: Poutsma--Jespersen--Kruisinga" in Zandvoort 1970d: 85-97.

---. (1970b) "Grammatical Terminology" in Zandvoort 1970d: 97-109.

---. (1970c) "Is 'Aspect' an English Verbal Category?" in Zandvoort 1970d: 109-126.

---. (1970d) <u>Collected Papers II</u>. Groningen: Wolters-Noordhoff.

Summary of Contents

This dissertation deals with the problem of representing ways of referring to the future that are available to the speaker of British English. The description under discussion is not viewed as a sample of theoretical grammar testing out one particular linguistic theory but as a sample of pedagogical grammar, that is, the description of a language designing a use in language teaching. Due to the relative novelty of designing a grammar from the start as a pedagogical description per se it is necessary to spell out in more than a cursory manner the principles on which such a grammar should be based. The aim of the dissertation as expressed in the title thus naturally permits of two subdivisions, each dependent on the other. Firstly we must ask ourselves how should a pedagogical grammar be designed and secondly give a sample of such a grammar to demonstrate the principles we have established. In this case the sample deals with the extremely controversial area of future reference and more particularly with verbal forms of future reference since these lie at the heart of the controversy. Hopefully the approach outlined in the dissertation will enable the teacher and learner of English to view this area more coherently.

A pedagogical grammar should be more than a simplification of more theoretical descriptions. Even if it were just a matter of simplification, many factors would need to be considered as to how and what to simplify. In other words, simplification in itself is hardly a simple matter. It is however worthwhile to approach the problem in something other than a parasitic way as if linguistic description should dominate the design and

other pedagogical considerations should only play a minor role. The
pedagogical grammarian should select not only from linguistics but also
from psychology and sociology just those aspects which suit him. In fact
a pedagogical grammar should be more based on psychological principles
than on any of the current, established linguistic theories. The way we
learn a language system must direct the way we set out language
descriptions for the learner; even a pedagogical grammar in the sense of
a comprehensive reference book should be designed so that the learner
and materials writer can use it in an optimal manner. It should be
consumer-oriented. Although learning theory is in the same kind of turmoil
as linguistic theory, it is now possible to say that the behaviourist
school has fallen short of everyone's expectations. The reduction of
learning to stimulus and response has ignored the internal organising
processes of the mind and explained little about human as opposed to
animal learning. In the same way the very real contribution of structural
linguistics which has been associated with behaviourist psychology has
not enabled us to explain the phenomena of language in anything but a
very narrow and limited sphere. Much has been written concerning the
formal structure of language but as to the study of meaning there has been
a general avoidance of what threatens to be an area where it is impossible
to say anything objective and systematic. But the expression of meanings
is precisely what at least the language learner-and teacher-wants to know
about. There is psychological evidence from the cognitive school of
psychology that meaning should form the basis of a pedagogical grammar.
David Ausubel, the educational psychologist, stresses that it is precisely
meaningful learning, where the learner relates new information to

information already in the mind that distinguishes human and animal
learning behaviour whereas rote learning i.e. learning new information
in an arbitrary and verbatim way without any organisation is shared by
both man and the lower animals. Meaningfully learned material is learned
better and retained longer and teaching programmes that use the
principles of meaningful learning are better than those that stress the
unconscious automatic acquisition of new responses. Meaningful
learning requires that the learner understands what he is learning. This
understanding can be facilitated by the use of so-called "organisers"
which first prepare the learner in a broad abstract manner for the
acquisition of new concepts and then relate these concepts as they are
introduced to previously learned concepts. Accordingly the pedagogical
description of future reference introduces the overall concept of
referring to the future and then provides a systematic network of
subconcepts based on this superordinate idea. In this way we avoid the
dilemma of a formal structural approach to English which may account for
the syntactic behaviour of various verbals in various parts of the
description but which does not bring together in a systematic way those
forms which express related meanings, in this case that of future
reference. It is not of interest to the learner that English has no
"future tense" formally speaking. This formal statement is irrelevant
to his real need to express certain meanings, to refer to the future,
to know how in English it is possible to talk about events occurring after
the present moment. The notional approach allows us to make a clear
distinction between _tense_, the formal syntactic category, and the notion
of _time_ or time reference. A pedagogical grammar should provide a

systematic picture of the different notions of time reference. The syntactic behaviour of forms can be listed and described in a separate and subordinate section of the grammar. With respect to future reference in English, two basic subnotions may be expressed: that of the Future-Future and the Present-Future. The Future-Future enables the speaker to view the future state or event as relating only to the future, the not-now (or not-yet). The Present-Future links the state or event with something in the present, either something imminent, in the process of happening or something that is programmed in some way as in the case of a personal or mutual decision, or a wide scale plan or timetable. These two concepts serve as organisers for the introduction of further subconcepts, namely the real and projected future-future and the general versus the formal and informal types of programmed Present-Future. Finally English allows us a Combined View as in <u>I'll be driving into town anyway</u> where there is the idea of a program already in existence but which is more related to a future event, e.g. giving somebody a lift, than to the present.